Mr. Notre Dame

Slim,
I hope this book about my Dad
brings back many great memories
of Notre Dame and the many times
that you where together in New
York City with the "Moose". We
appreciate your loyalty to the
Notre Dame Spirit.

Mary Krause Carrigan

Phil Krause

Slim — I was 5 years old when
you graduated, (with Dads help?)
Thanks for all you did for him &
Coach Leahy at the end of the war
(See Chpt. 4)   Fr Ed Krause, C.S.C.

Mr. Notre Dame

The Life and Legend of
Edward "Moose" Krause

JASON KELLY

To Slim —
One of the fortunate people
who knew Moose well. I hope this
book brings back fond memories
Best wishes,
Jason Kelly

DIAMOND COMMUNICATIONS

A Member of the Rowman & Littlefield Publishing Group

Lanham ✦ South Bend ✦ New York ✦ Oxford

Published by Diamond Communications
A Member of the Rowman & Littlefield Publishing Group
4720 Boston Way
Lanham, Maryland 20706

Distributed by National Book Network

Library of Congress Cataloging-in-Publication Data

Kelly, Jason, 1972-
    Mr. Notre Dame : the life and legend of Edward "Moose" Krause /
Jason Kelly.
        p. cm.
    ISBN 1-888698-40-3 (Cloth : alk. paper)
    1. Krause, Edward, 1913–1992. 2. Athletic directors—United States—
Biography. 3. Basketball coaches—United States—Biography. 4. University
of Notre Dame—Sports—History. I. Title: Mister Notre Dame. II. Title.

GV697.K73 K45 2002
796.323'092 B—dc21   2002006510

⊖™ The paper used in this publication meets the minimum requirements of
American National Standard for Information Sciences—Permanence of
Paper for Printed Library Materials, ANSI/NISO Z39.48–1992.
Manufactured in the United States of America.

To Roland and Joyce Kelly

Contents

Acknowledgments

OPENING THEIR HOMES AND HEARTS, ALONG WITH many painful old wounds, the children of Edward "Moose" Krause made it possible to chronicle the true story of their father's life. They shared his tragedies as well as his triumphs in emotional detail that still inspires tears and laughter among them. Without their candor, this book would be no more than a glimpse back at the many glory days of Notre Dame athletics that Krause experienced as a player, coach and administrator. Perhaps that story, which spans the generations from Rockne to Holtz, would be worthy enough in itself to be the subject of a book. But that was his life's work, not his life story. Krause's children understand that better than anyone. Rev. Edward Krause described the difference in the eulogy he delivered for his father, saying "a love affair with the whole of life, with the energy and the mystery of it, that's what Dad's story is all about." He and his younger sister and brother, Mary Carrigan and Phil Krause, articulated that point in vivid and compelling stories that revealed why their father remains so revered on the Notre Dame campus and beyond.

They all share many of their father's traits, from his charismatic personality and sense of humor, to his ear for a good story, to his genetic incapability to say no. More than agreeing to my many requests for interviews and information, they invariably offered to give more. Not ten feet from where I'm sitting now, a stack of scrapbooks, personal letters and family photographs—precious material their mother, Elise, meticulously kept—serves as a virtual Library of Krause. They have never asked when this treasure trove of family memories would be returned, only if I needed anything else.

To Father Ed, Mary, Phil and their families: thank you for making it possible to tell this story so completely. Many other friends and colleagues of Krause offered similarly intimate glimpses from their own perspectives. Jack Connor, the author of *Leahy's Lads* and a natural storyteller, made 1940s football practices seem more vivid than a *SportsCenter* highlight. Jack's brother, George, the All-American tackle, met Krause when he was still selling sprinklers to Catholic parishes in Chicago. George idolized Krause then, and to hear his tone of voice when he talked about their relationship, that feeling remained sixty years and hundreds of victory cigars later. Marty O'Connor, a former Notre Dame basketball player and a polio victim who remembered his hospitalization down to the itchy blankets wrapped around him, cried when he discussed Krause's supportive presence at his bedside. And Joe Doyle, the former *South Bend Tribune* sports editor, made me feel the hangover from a bender that happened before I was born.

This list could go on and on—and, in a way, it does over the next couple hundred pages. Too many people contributed too many brushstrokes to this portrait of Krause to acknowledge any of them as fully as they deserve. I hope the story they helped tell serves as adequate thanks.

I also hope it is worth the sacrifices colleagues, friends and family made along the way. Jill Langford showed patience and encouragement to ease my anxiety about an unfamiliar business, while displaying a passion for the project and trust in my approach that inspired confidence. Bill Bilinski, the sports editor at the *South Bend Tribune,* also supported and accommodated me throughout this process, no matter the inconvenience to him. Bill and Eric Hansen, the managing editor of *Irish Sports Report,* both helped me carve enough time out of a reporter's quirky schedule to devote to this project without a whisper of complaint. Charles Lamb, Marlene Wasikowski and Erik Dix of the University of Notre Dame archives provided valuable assistance with audiovisual materials and photographs. Hearing Krause deliver a speech to Army chaplains in Europe or seeing him alongside Frank Leahy on the sidelines in an overcoat and a fedora in the 1940s brings the stories of those occasions vividly to life. The Notre Dame archives houses a wealth of similar material and its dedicated staff graciously shared it with me.

Finally, and most importantly, an inadequate thank you to my family, who often seemed more enthusiastic about this project than I did. I'm not certain where the idea to write a biography of Krause originated, but if it didn't start with my father, Roland, he kept it alive with his gentle prodding. I know he's as proud as anyone to see it finally in print. It never seemed to matter to my mother, Joyce, that I was writing a book—and I mean that as a compliment. If I wrote parking tickets for a living, she would be happy as long as I enjoyed it. That's a comforting feeling in a world where many people care more about resumes than relationships. Inspiration also comes from my sister, Laurie Dow, and her husband, Rick. They offer one generous gesture after another, large and small, too often taken for granted, but never forgotten. My brother, Randy, says I told him at age nine that I wanted to write a book. I'll take his word for it. Since that day, or at least as long as I can remember, he's assured me a hundred different ways that it—and anything else—is possible.

Nobody sacrificed more to make this book possible than my wife, Kara, who had to fit her life around my bizarre work habits. There must have been days when she wondered if it would ever be finished, but I never knew it. I know there were many days when I felt that way, and Kara provided the motivation to make sure that I would see it through to the end.

Foreword

FIRST HEARD OF MOOSE KRAUSE IN 1941 WHEN HE came to our house on the south side of Chicago to recruit my brother George to attend Holy Cross College where Moose was then a coach. I was in eighth grade at the time and I remember when he walked in the door, he was so big he blocked the whole doorway. I wasn't sure who he was at the time, but I learned about him the following year when I was a freshman at DeLaSalle High School. I learned about Moose's Lithuanian roots; that Moose and his brother Phil were the stars on D's athletic teams in the late 1920s; and that Moose went on to star in football and basketball at Notre Dame. Our athletic director, Brother Austin, talked about Moose every chance he could during my four years at DeLaSalle. I not only learned of Moose's prowess in football and basketball but also of his prodigious appetite and his endearing charm. It seems he could talk the Brothers into or out of anything. He became a larger than life figure to me.

My next encounter with Moose was when I reported to summer football practice at Notre Dame in 1946. He was an assistant football

coach in charge of the tackles under Frank Leahy and also the head basketball coach. I saw Moose every day on the practice field that fall and
many times up close, as our freshman group scrimmaged the varsity
often. I was impressed with Moose's demeanor on the field. He never
hollered or even raised his voice. He had such a presence about him that
he didn't have to raise his voice to make a point. When he wanted to
correct a mistake a player made he would tell the player straight out
what he did wrong and then how to do it the right way. He never belit-
tled a player no matter what mistake was made. Moose made it a point
to compliment a player when it was called for and when you heard him
say, "That's the way to tackle" or "Good block," it made you feel like a
million dollars because it came from Moose.

Moose had a charm about him that is hard to describe. He seemed
to have a perpetual twinkle in his eye that signaled that he was at peace
with himself and the world around him. He was the type of person who
was fun to be around. I'm sure Moose got angry at times, but I never
saw him when he was upset. He was one of the most even-tempered
persons I was ever around.

One day as an underclassman at Notre Dame, I was walking across
the campus with John Lujack, one of the stars of the football team, and
we encountered Moose. He smiled and said in that warm voice of his,
"Hi Jack (to me)–good to see you Sheriff" (to Lujack). Some time later
I was again with one of the stars of the team and met Moose. The
greeting from Moose was the same–I was called by name and the other
one "Sheriff." I figured out that his pet name for a player who "made it"
was Sheriff. I can remember thinking how terrific it would be to get to
the point where I would merit that lofty status of being called "Sheriff"
by Moose. In my senior year I, along with a sophomore teammate, were
approaching the athletic offices when we saw Moose. He called out, "Hi
Bob (to my teammate)–good to see you Sheriff" (to me). I couldn't
believe it–I was called by his pet name. I had arrived.

Years later I found out that Moose took great pride in calling the football and basketball players by name but found it difficult to remember the names of so many of the athletes who had graduated as they returned to campus. In his own clever way he devised a plan. He would make it a point to learn the athletes names and call them by name during their early years at school. When they became seniors he switched to calling them "Sheriff." Then in the years that followed, when he saw one of the former players he wouldn't have to scramble to recall the name; he would call out, "Sheriff, it's good to see you back." When I learned this, it made Moose all the more endearing to think he went to this length so as to not offend anyone by not remembering their name. It was so typical of Moose.

Other than the Grotto, Moose's office was the most visited place on campus, particularly by former ballplayers. Moose was everyone's favorite. He was a delight to be with whether it was visiting in his office, on the golf course or in his booth—one of the wooden booths on the roof of the old stadium where he was at his best. He would invite former teammates, his favorite friends, family members and former players to share the booth with him to watch the Notre Dame home football games. It was considered a great honor to be invited by Moose to sit in his booth. My brother George, who stayed close to Moose through the years, was a permanent member, as was Creighton Miller, the Hall of Fame back from the 1943 Notre Dame team. When Moose heard I was writing a book, *Leahy's Lads,* I became a regular visitor in the booth.

George and I agree that those times spent with Moose in his booth over the course of three seasons were some of the happiest and most fun times of our lives. Moose was the perfect host and also a benevolent dictator in his booth. He ordered all his guests to arrive early so as to have more time for storytelling. He told us where to sit and then the fun began, as Moose would start the proceedings in the same way by saying, "George, tell them about the time I recruited you" or "tell them about my instructions to you in the Iowa game" or whatever story he wanted to hear. George could always get Moose to laugh when he told the group the story of Moose reporting to Knute Rockne for the first time. According to George, Rockne asked Moose what number he wanted. Moose replied, "number 69." When asked why, Moose was reported as saying, "So I'll have the same number whether I'm standing up or upside down." And Creighton Miller could make Moose laugh uproariously no matter how many times he told the story of Moose being asked by a reporter before a football game, "Coach, how many men are you going to dress?" According to Creighton, Moose replied, "I am going to dress 22, the rest will have to dress themselves."

Moose always lit one of his big cigars when we arrived in the booth. Our final year in the booth was the year they banned smoking in the stadium. The head usher spotted Moose with his lit cigar and went immediately to Dick Rosenthal's booth and informed him, as the athletic director, that Moose Krause was smoking in his booth. Rosenthal said to the usher, "That's Moose Krause. He can do whatever he wants." During one of the games that year we were visited in the booth by Father Ted Hesburgh, the president emeritus of Notre Dame. He greeted all of us warmly and was invited by Moose to sit next to him. The two old friends were enjoying each other's company when Father Hesburgh pulled a cigar from his pocket and said, "I understand you smoke in this booth. Is it all right if I light up?" I think that speaks volumes about Moose's legendary status at Notre Dame, when Notre Dame's most famous president asks Moose for permission to smoke in the stadium.

When Moose died, it was a terrible blow to all who knew him. As George and I say, "we lost a father, a brother, a confidant and best friend all rolled into one." In memory of Moose, I wrote a poem about him and our days with him in his booth called "In Heaven with Moose," which is engraved on a bronze plaque and housed in the Moose section in the Joyce Athletic Center. He was truly a legend and a remarkable man. We still miss him.

When I heard Jason Kelly was writing a book about Moose's life I was thrilled. Although there have been books written about Moose, none seemed to have done him justice; a good book about Moose was needed. Jason, as the son of my classmate Roland Kelly, grew up learning of the traditions and mystique of that special place called Notre Dame and of one of its legends, Moose Krause. I was sure Jason would write the book from a unique perspective.

When I read the manuscript it was all that I hoped for and more. Jason has captured Moose as few have done by blending amusing stories with insights into Moose's character and personality. *Mr. Notre Dame* is much more than a story of a young man who rose from humble Lithuanian roots to become a Notre Dame legend. It is also a story of a man who, by his charm and strong character, endeared himself to all who knew him, from the thousands of students he encountered along the way to fellow athletic directors, coaches and captains of industry. I wholeheartedly recommend *Mr. Notre Dame* to all readers who would like to know such a man.

GEORGE CONNOR AND JACK CONNOR

Introduction

FROM *KNUTE ROCKNE ALL-AMERICAN* TO *RUDY,* THE stories of Notre Dame's athletic legends have captured the imagination of millions. Yet the life story of Edward "Moose" Krause, the man eulogized in the *New York Times* as the "true legend" of Notre Dame, has never been fully told. That's probably his fault. Plenty of people encouraged him to write his memoirs, but he always begged off, preferring to deflect attention and credit for his half-century of service to the university. When one of his successors as athletic director, Dick Rosenthal, worked out the details for Krause to write a book with best-selling author Stephen Singular, the title above the big "MOOSE KRAUSE" byline suggested it would not be a revealing autobiography. It was called *Notre Dame's Greatest Coaches*—of which Krause was not one—and it chronicled the careers of Rockne, Leahy, Parseghian and Holtz, the men who built and maintained the Irish football tradition.

Singular deftly incorporated many of the details of Krause's life into the book, interweaving it with the highs and lows of decades of Notre Dame football. Had Krause not died just weeks after the 1992 season featured in the book, the final version probably would have included less of his own life. It's a richer text with Krause's story sprinkled throughout it, just as Notre Dame's athletic history is richer for his vast contributions.

Few would argue with a slight editing of the title of that book to make it apply directly to Krause: "Notre Dame's Greatest." It may sound like hyperbole, but the love and admiration for Krause, still palpable nearly a decade after his death, suggests few have accomplished more or generated as much goodwill for Notre Dame. No less a legend than Rev. Theodore M. Hesburgh, president emeritus of the university and its most respected leader of the last fifty years, says, "If I ever met a saint, he was one of them."

What inspires such effusive praise? Not the fact that Krause, an All-American in football and basketball, stands as the greatest Notre Dame athlete of his time and one of the best ever. Not his brief stints as a football assistant and head basketball coach during one of the most prosperous periods in Fighting Irish history in the 1940s and '50s. Not even his thirty years as athletic director, a distinguished tenure but hardly a path to canonization. No, Krause holds an exalted place in Notre Dame history for achievements that cannot be quantified, for a generosity of spirit and strength of character in the face of harrowing challenges. When his wife, Elise, suffered injuries so serious in a car accident that death may have been the most merciful result, Krause cared for her with the gentle patience of the parent of a newborn. He fed her and carried her up and down the stairs of their home for months until she regained some semblance of strength. Mentally, she never recovered. Krause endured verbal assaults from Elise, whose brain damage permanently altered her personality. He took the abuse with the understanding that it was just her injuries talking.

Krause suffered festering injuries of his own in the wake of his wife's accident. Always a social drinker on the convention and speaking circuit, Krause became an alcoholic. He took bottles of scotch to Elise's hospital room, where he sang her to sleep and drank himself into a stupor. It went on that way for years, Krause taking care his wife even when he could not take care of himself. To those who knew Krause best, his fundamental nature never changed. He remained generous to a fault, a sought-after speaker with an ear for comic timing, a living icon who connected Notre Dame's storied past to its present. Yet the day-to-day details of his job became increasingly difficult to handle. Krause's assistant and dearest friend in the last years of his life, Col. Jack Stephens, covered for him in every sense of the term.

Friends and family tried to help Krause, alternately consoling and confronting him, trying to awaken him to the damage he was inflicting. He summoned the will to stop only after heart problems he compounded with his drinking left him unconscious on a hospital stretcher requiring shock treatments to survive. At the brink of death, Krause's alcoholism came to a screeching halt. As abruptly as the accident that triggered his descent, Krause recovered and became an active sponsor for Alcoholics Anonymous. He counseled several friends who felt ashamed of their disease but comfortable attending AA meetings in Krause's office.

Krause had a way of making people feel comfortable. His candor about his own struggles allowed people to relate to him on an intimate level, to feel like they shared something with this legend at once larger than life and humbled by it. Religion rooted Krause in the belief that a greater victory awaited him than any athletic or professional achievement.

Krause could have had more money and power—he never made more than $30,000 a year at Notre Dame and deferred all high-profile decisions to Hesburgh and Executive Vice President Edmund P. Joyce. Yet he felt he owed Notre Dame for the opportunity it provided him as a kid from the gritty streets around the Chicago stockyards without much hope of ever seeing the world beyond them. It's a debt he paid many times over.

Few have embodied the hard-to-define "Notre Dame spirit" as well as Krause. It does not mean victory necessarily, but the pursuit of victory "though the odds be great or small," the belief that success can be achieved no matter the obstacles. It does not mean infallibility at all, but the recognition of human frailty and the constant struggle for the discipline to overcome that and accomplish a greater good.

Krause applied the lessons of athletics to life and believed sports played an integral role in the educational process. He spent his life trying to make that available to everyone from the greatest Notre Dame quarterback to the elementary school novice. He served for thirty-five years as the chairman of the South Bend Parks and Recreation Commission, lobbying for funds and facilities and events to enrich the sporting life of the community.

Winning and losing didn't matter too much to Krause, though his fidgety demeanor in his private box high above Notre Dame Stadium on football Saturdays may have suggested otherwise. He cared about competition that formed character and camaraderie that formed lasting relationships. Both sustained Krause through challenges far greater than a fourth-and-long play.

That Krause faced those challenges and prevailed made him the man they call "Mr. Notre Dame" more than any of his athletic exploits. If life itself had a final score, Krause certainly would be counted among the biggest winners. As his son, Rev. Edward Krause, said in his eulogy: "It wouldn't be important that he, like Peter in the Gospel, may not always have succeeded. Jesus himself, of course, by purely worldly standards could only be counted a failure. No, what is important is that he, coach that he was, never stopped playing with all his heart and bulk. He fought, as Paul says in the epistle, to the finish line, right up to the final whistle, a Notre Dame trait if ever there was one."

✦ ✦ ✦

Moose Krause has been memorialized in bronze on the Notre Dame campus with a statue as approachable as the man himself. Sculptor Jerry McKenna seated Krause casually on a bench, his ever-present cigar in his left hand and his right arm draped out as if inviting you to join him. Across the street, Frank Leahy's statue—like his stature in life—has been placed on a pedestal, above the masses. It's a tableau that represents their personalities and their immeasurable contributions to Notre Dame athletic lore. Leahy, mad scientist of the sidelines, watches from above, a looming presence prodding the Irish toward perfection. And Krause, jovial ambassador, gazes toward the coach with admiration as he beckons you over to tell you about the time. If you sit down next to Krause, he'll tell you some stories, but probably not much about himself, even though that may be the best story of all.

Back of the Yards

AMID THE SOUND OF LOWING CATTLE AND GRUNT-
ing pigs, clattering streetcars and locomotive whis-
tles, the hard consonants of eastern Europe
echoed along the crowded avenues of Chicago's Back of the Yards
neighborhood. A steady stream of immigrants from Czechoslovakia,
Poland and Lithuania arrived at the turn of the twentieth century, seeking economic opportunity and religious freedom in America. They
found little more than dangerous, low-wage work in the stockyards and
meatpacking plants. Upton Sinclair described the inhumane working
conditions and abject poverty of the neighborhood in his novel *The
Jungle*, the story of a Lithuanian family struggling to survive in a culture
they did not understand.

A patchwork of traditions coexisted within "Packingtown," which
stretched south from 39th to 55th streets with Ashland Avenue as the
clogged artery at its heart. With blocks divided along ethnic lines almost
as defined as Europe itself, many immigrants tried to maintain their heritage with customs imported from home. At this clamorous intersection

of the agrarian ideal and the industrial revolution, though, the disorienting noise of daily life drowned out almost everything else.

"This awesome medley represented economic vitality and wealth as
well as survival through day labor," Thomas Jablonsky writes in *Pride in the
Jungle: Community and Everyday Life in Back of the Yards Chicago.* "The yards,
in essence, conditioned the nature of everyday life for nearby residents."

Smokestacks from the surrounding meat-packing plants belched
sooty exhaust, "thick, oily and black as night," as Sinclair described it in *The
Jungle.* It gave the neighborhood a foul odor and its inhabitants a gray, dour
cast. But they kept coming, as if following the scent. It reeked of available
labor. As Sinclair's Rudkus family approached the neighborhood, the
oppressive smell became overpowering: "It was no longer something far
off and faint, that you caught in whiffs; you could literally taste it. . . . It
was an elemental odor, raw and crude; it was rich, almost rancid, sensual,
and strong. There were some who drank it in as if it were an intoxicant."

Walter and Theresa Krauciunas arrived in the Back of the Yards
from Lithuania in the years after Sinclair's literary indictment appeared
in 1906. They found living and working conditions less threatening than
those exposed in *The Jungle,* but they still struggled to make a living.
Settling at 4614 South Paulina in what Sinclair described as a "wilder-
ness of two-story frame tenements . . . where architecture is a luxury
that is dispensed with," Walter and Theresa opened a butcher shop on
the ground floor of their utilitarian two-flat.

Dozens of similar businesses dotted the concrete landscape, serving tiny fractions of the community. By 1910, more than 100 Lithuanian-
owned businesses had sprung up in the Back of the Yards, catering
primarily to neighbors within a one-block radius. That intimacy with
their customers moved most of the business owners to extend credit, or
outright charity, in difficult economic times. It was a custom imported
from Lithuania, "a tradition of helping neighbors and of collective assistance . . . sympathy or solidarity with one's neighbors was widespread

among the Lithuanians," David Fainhauz writes in *Lithuanians in the USA: Aspects of Ethnic Identity*. They called it *talka*. This tradition may have kept the immigrant community close-knit, but it also led to the bankruptcy of many of the most generous businesses after the stock market crash of 1929 spread poverty like a virus.

Years before the Depression cut its destructive swath, the growing Krauciunas family built a vibrant, albeit modest, life in America. Walter and Theresa's second child, Edward Walter Krauciunas, was born on February 2, 1913, into a family cash-poor but spirit-rich. Ed's childhood friends remember his father as a gregarious and generous man who joked with them and fed them whenever they visited. Less adept with English, Theresa had more difficulty communicating, but the smell of baking bread from one of her favorite Lithuanian recipes created a warm and inviting atmosphere.

By 1918, four children filled their four-room flat—Philip, the oldest, Ed and younger sisters Harriet and Bernice. They had no toilet in the house, navigating around chicken coops and Doberman droppings in the backyard to get to the outhouse. Once a week, Walter took his sons to a nearby tavern to bathe in the back room.

In a neighborhood known for breaking spirits—a two-block stretch of Ashland Avenue had so many taverns where men dulled the mental and physical pain of their existence, it became known as Whiskey Row—Walter and Theresa wanted their children to find strength in faith. Holy Cross parish became the spiritual and educational center of the children's lives, along with most of the Lithuanian Catholic community. Phil and Ed served as altar boys for Sunday Mass and attended elementary school at Holy Cross. Through everyday trials and staggering tragedies, the rituals of the Catholic Church served as the foundation that supported them.

Their youngest sister, Bernice, died in 1924 at age six. Though the specifics of her illness faded from Ed's memory over time, he never forgot the solace the family found in faith. Even as a young boy, he felt its healing power and he sought the comfort of Gospel readings and Communion wafers throughout his life in good times and bad.

Walter and Theresa also exposed their children to the Lithuanian language and classical music at home, an attempt to pass on the traditions of the land they fled. They allowed Phil and Ed to roam over to nearby Davis Square Park for football and baseball games with their friends, but they insisted the boys take music lessons to develop the cultural appreciation they brought with them from Lithuania. It didn't take. Ed would tell stories of walking to violin lessons through surrounding neighborhoods, dodging snowballs and insults, and literally fighting for his reputation while carrying an instrument the other kids considered feminine. "First, the Irish kids would beat me up," he says in his book, *Notre Dame's Greatest Coaches,* written with Stephen Singular. "Then the Italians took a whack at me. And then the Poles. By the time I got home, I knew how to box."

That memory hints at the influences tugging at the American-born children of immigrants. Respect among peers in the Back of the Yards meant displaying toughness, not talent with an instrument. It meant gathering with the guys for games in the park and throwing a few punches, when necessary, to defend your friends, your teammates and your honor. Those childhood marks of distinction transcended ethnic tensions and diminished, in their minds at least, the traditions their parents tried to teach. It made them Americans.

Ed received his introduction to sports from an uncle, Jack Mason, a former middleweight boxer. Mason took his six-year-old nephew on a train trip to Toledo, where he saw Jack Dempsey defeat Jess Willard for the heavyweight championship in 1919. Ed returned with stars in his eyes. It fueled his dreams of being a participant in such a spectacle someday.

A few years later, Ed and a group of friends sneaked into Soldier Field in Chicago to see a football game between Notre Dame and

Southern California. In just the second game of a series that would become one of the most enduring and intense intersectional rivalries in college football, the Irish won 7-6 and Ed "started dreaming about going to Notre Dame."

Ed did not deny Walter and Theresa's wishes entirely. He quit violin, but took up clarinet to placate them, practicing at home alongside Phil at the piano. By their own admission, their rehearsals annoyed the neighbors. As musicians, apparently, they were developing into excellent athletes. Still, they studied their instruments for several years. Ed even entered high school at Chicago's famed DeLaSalle Institute with plans to play in the marching band. Yet he loved nothing more than his hours in the park, where he showed off his burgeoning athletic ability. Walter and Theresa tolerated this intrusion into chores like homework, practicing his clarinet and working in the butcher shop, even if they did not understand the appeal.

Above all, Walter and Theresa expected their children to work. In the most literal sense, their shop became a family business. Chickens strutted and clucked in their backyard coops, to be plucked for sale alongside the sausage and cuts of meat that left their hands and arms bloodied from the preparation. When they heard Theresa's whistle, Phil and Ed ambled reluctantly home from whatever game had diverted their attention that day. They rolled up their sleeves and soon found themselves up to their elbows in raw meat.

Walter awakened before dawn most mornings with the rest of the grocers and butchers to purchase produce and meat from the wholesale markets in the Loop, the only way to keep fresh and cheap goods in stock. He returned with enough for a day or a week and opened the store with the Dobermans at his side for protection from the neighborhood's prevalent criminal element. While certainly not a thriving business, the butcher shop kept the family fed and woven into the fabric of the neighborhood.

Walter gave freely, whether people needed it or not. When hard times hit the neighbors, they could count on having enough meat and milk and eggs without worrying about their bill. When their children's friends stopped in, they were greeted with a big smile, a warm hello and sandwiches with thick cuts of ham and roast beef. Phil and Ed often went to school with a sack full of sandwiches to share with friends. Sometimes they wouldn't even wait until lunchtime to indulge, sneaking the sandwiches into their classrooms and lifting up their desktops to hide as they stole a bite.

Ed's ample eating habits fueled his already advanced physical development, aided by strenuous summer jobs in the stockyards. Though awkward on his feet as an adolescent, he clearly had a frame built for football, even if his parents still tried to disavow him of that notion. They encouraged Ed to pursue a spot in the marching band when he enrolled at DeLaSalle High School. He intended to do that, even participating in rehearsals until football coach Norm Barry spotted him.

Barry's reputation preceded him among the boys at DeLaSalle. He had played alongside the legendary George Gipp in the backfield for Notre Dame's 1920 national championship football team. While coaching at DeLaSalle, Barry also coached the professional Chicago Cardinals to a league title and worked as a lawyer. He represented all the opportunities athletics and education opened to the boys of DeLaSalle. They revered Barry and envisioned themselves following in his footsteps someday.

Impressed with Ed's size, Barry encouraged him to give football a try. Ed did not need much prodding, but his commitment to the band and his parents' wishes stood in the way. DeLaSalle's band leader, Brother Basil, told Ed he had to choose between the two extracurricular activities. His parents realized they were fighting a futile battle. With their grudging permission, Ed left his clarinet on the shelf to gather dust and pulled out his cleats to collect mud.

✦ ✦ ✦

DeLaSalle loomed. Already a Chicago institution for almost forty years when Ed arrived in 1926, the imposing four-story building—and the black-clad Christian Brothers who ruled it—struck fear into the hearts of the student body. It also offered an opportunity, the magnitude of which the students did not fully appreciate until their high school experience faded into romantic memory. As alumnus Bill Granger observed in a 1979 *Chicago Tribune* article, it served "as a sort of finishing school for the rough Irish, Italian, Polish and Lithuanian Catholic boys who streamed out of the dirty tenements . . . and took an education like a man taking a trade. DeLaSalle for them became a sort of street-smart playing fields of Eton."

When Ed rode the trolley for his first day at DeLaSalle on September 7, 1926, with his clarinet and his class schedule, he could not have envisioned a future for himself beyond the boundaries of the Back of the Yards. Ed may have dreamed of playing football for Notre Dame like all the other Catholic boys with a radio and an imagination. As inclined toward spirituality as sports, a dream of becoming pope would have seemed no less realistic.

In burly Brother John, DeLaSalle's disciplinarian, Ed first saw devout Catholicism and virile athleticism coexist. A former sparring partner of heavyweight boxing champion Jim Corbett, Brother John maintained good behavior among the boys with fear and, failing that, physical force. As Ed's stature and status grew in his high school years, he became a big man on campus in every sense of the term. Brother John made sure he never got too big. Ed and his friend Harold Shean, a fellow hulking tackle on the football team, occasionally exploited their physical power and popularity in the lunchroom. "We lorded over things a little bit, pushing guys out of the way a little bit," Shean says. "Brother John, with one fell swoop, knocked the both of us on our butts."

Ed often suffered a similar fate on the football field as a freshman, struggling to master the nuances of the game and control his gangly body. Smaller players maneuvered over and around him at the line of scrimmage, frustrating Barry, who finally barked one day, "You're big enough to be a moose and you can't even block that little guy!" The nickname stuck. Barry also shortened the hard-to-pronounce Krauciunas to Krause on the practice field. As a circuit court judge in Chicago a few years later, Barry made that change official in the eyes of the law.

At DeLaSalle, Moose Krause made a name for himself. He grew into a commanding physical force, yet he maintained agility unusual in that era among athletes of his size. Once the rest of his body caught up with his oversized feet and ungainly limbs, Krause developed an ability not only to overpower smaller opponents, but to outmaneuver them as well. At 6-foot-3, 230 pounds, he cast an imposing shadow over the competitive Chicago Catholic league in football and basketball.

Colliding with opposing linemen to clear running room for higher-profile players on the football field, his sheer power obscured his deft footwork. On the basketball court, "he had more moves than a burlesque dancer—honest to God," classmate Don Herron says. Planted beneath the basket with no threat of the modern-day three-second violation to budge him from the lane, Krause became an immovable object—until he got the ball. Then he would pivot and head-fake and dribble and spin, looking for a guard streaking toward the basket or a clear shot for himself.

DeLaSalle's domination in basketball extended beyond Chicago. Krause led the team to two consecutive national Catholic championships. Future college teammate John Ford's team from Indianapolis Cathedral High tried to dethrone Krause and DeLaSalle during one national tournament in Chicago. Ford preferred to be on Krause's side. "He was a supreme pivotman, just a master," Ford says. "Everything centered around him."

Krause's rare combination of size and agility—along with the bit of good fortune that his coach, Norm Barry, had played football under Knute Rockne at Notre Dame—would earn him a college scholarship. Rockne recruited through a network of former players and other Notre Dame alumni who scouted talent for him in their hometowns. Barry referred his star lineman to the iconic Irish coach. His opinion carried particular weight with Rockne because of Barry's success in coaching. Barry escorted Krause to South Bend in the spring of 1930 to make a formal introduction to Rockne. "It was like meeting God," Krause said. "That was one of the most exciting moments of my life, and I knew right away I wanted to come to Notre Dame."

Ed's parents felt no such awe for a football coach; they did not understand the game or the increasing fascination Americans had for its heroes. A college education still seemed impractical to immigrant parents, who often felt disconnected from the cultural opportunities available to their children in America. As suitable as Ed's muscular frame seemed for a football career, he appeared equally well-built for a life of stockyard labor. A paycheck, however meager, would be an immediate benefit to the family. A degree from Notre Dame, little more than an abstraction in his parents' minds, promised nothing. Free room and board, however, along with Notre Dame's Catholic identity, persuaded Walter and Theresa to give their blessing to the academic and athletic pursuits Ed craved.

An Athlete and a Gentleman

PRIESTS CLOAKED IN BLACK CASSOCKS RULED Notre Dame like a sectarian Supreme Court, though they seldom listened to opposing arguments before rendering a decision. They imposed strict rules that kept daily life as orderly as possible from the 6:30 A.M. wake-up bell until lights out at 11 o'clock. Four days out of five, students were required to attend chapel service, and they were expected to be in class even more religiously. Any absences were duly noted and discouraged with punishments swift and stern. At meals, a group of priests sat on a raised platform at the end of the dining hall, their authoritative presence prominent at even the most mundane moments. "Ten CSCs. All in their habits and their birettas," Krause's classmate Vince McAloon says. "They looked formidable."

Students looked less formidable, though no less formal, attending classes in jackets and ties. "We took pride in showing off our haberdashery," McAloon says. "Some fellows would come to class with a different outfit on every day, showing they had quite a wardrobe." In dire economic circumstances, many barely had a change of clothes, so they swapped with their friends to give themselves the natty appearance of a clotheshorse. It was one of their few connections to the material world beyond the campus boundaries.

Austere Notre Dame offered its students little in the way of creature comforts. During the Depression, what little they had was a welcome respite from the grim reality gripping the nation. When Ed Krause arrived in 1930, almost a year after the stock market crash paralyzed the economy, students appreciated three meals a day and a warm bed. It was more than some of them had at home. "I went through four years here in the depths of the Depression," McAloon says, "and I didn't realize it."

Nobody could be completely insulated from the insidious effects of the Depression. Even on campus, they were evident. Students regularly disappeared, forced to return home after their fathers lost their jobs, or worse, in the crushing economic wake. "Every day you went to class and there were fellows missing from the class. . . . It was right and left, it was like an epidemic," McAloon says. "It was so common that we didn't pay that much attention."

As students disappeared, other young men appeared, looking for friends from their hometowns, hoping to find something to eat and a place to sleep before returning to the road or the rails in search of work. "All sorts of characters appeared on campus. . . . I can remember dozens and dozens of them," McAloon says. "They belonged to the hobo generation."

Even scholarship athletes had to work for their room and board. Krause served as a waiter in the dining hall, wearing a crisp white jacket with a towel draped over his arm. He considered himself fortunate for the opportunity to work for his tuition, but he also discovered a way to make his labor a little more lucrative. He passed a hat. "For some reason," Krause said in *Notre Dame's Greatest Coaches*, "people dropped money into it." That helped pay for movies and milkshakes in his spare time, not that he had much as a multisport athlete at Notre Dame.

Krause stood out among hundreds of freshmen football hopefuls ineligible for the varsity but eager to attract Rockne's attention. His size alone would have set him apart from the masses spread across the scruffy practice turf just east of the newly built, red-brick Notre Dame Stadium. As one of the chosen delivered by Rockne's informal network of recruiters, Krause drew special notice. His high school football experience under Norm Barry had been a primer on Rockne's techniques, so he had an additional head start, as if his strength and dexterity did not give him enough of an advantage. Al Grisanti, a 155-pound senior lineman in 1930, recounted Rockne's reaction to Krause's obvious skill in *Notre Dame's Greatest Coaches*. "I was there when Rockne got his first look at Moose. His eyes lit up," Grisanti says. "He'd never seen anyone so big who could move that fast and that intelligently."

"Ed 'Moose' Krause was the first big man I had seen whose size was natural for him," Rockne's line coach Heartley "Hunk" Anderson writes in his memoir, *Notre Dame, Chicago Bears and Hunk*. "Moose was well coordinated and had strength as well as agility. He probably could have played in the backfield and I'll bet he would have given a good account of himself."

Krause's conspicuous presence on campus and on the football field did cause him some trouble as a freshman. In a story he told on himself to describe Rockne's influence in his life, Krause confronted a biology professor about a poor grade on an exam. He received a 30 on the test, but insisted he deserved much better. After the professor refused to look at it for possible grading errors, Krause went to the dean of the science department, who supported the professor's stance. In a fit of fury, Krause literally lifted the dean off the ground and pushed him against the wall. "Pack your bags," the dean told him, "and be off campus in two hours."

Stopping at Rockne's office on his way out of town to apologize and say good-bye, Krause got a reprieve and lecture instead. At once stern and reassuring, disappointed and understanding, Rockne extolled the virtues of respect for authority and emotional restraint. Still an apprehensive freshman, Krause sat in awe of his celebrated coach, whose charisma transcended his rotund figure and metallic voice. At the peak of his power on campus, Rockne promised to smooth things over with the dean if Krause learned to control his temper, especially when faced with such a situation. Rockne exerting his influence in such disciplinary situations, and other issues involving football players, caused some conflict with the administration, but in this case it preserved Krause's academic and athletic career.

It turned out he got a 78 on the biology exam, and though he failed the test of his composure and maturity afterward, he internalized a lesson that would last a lifetime. Krause often referred to Rockne's advice in the wake of that incident as the inspiration for his easygoing demeanor. "He taught me how to manage myself," Krause said in *Notre Dame's Greatest Coaches*, "and I never forgot that."

Krause displayed none of that restraint on the football field. Playing offensive and defensive tackle against the varsity during practice, he showed his elders no deference. "I had to scrimmage against Moose, the big bastard," Grisanti says, lamenting the fact that he never earned a monogram at Notre Dame. "He was scared to death as a freshman, but I took all the abuse. Everyone wondered why I couldn't get anywhere in football—it was because I had to block Moose Krause."

Grisanti was not the only varsity lineman who could not block Krause. During the week before Notre Dame's annual game against Army in 1930, Krause broke through the first-team offensive line and knocked star quarterback Frank Carideo out cold. Rockne hustled to Carideo's side and helped shake loose the cobwebs. He was a little wobbly, but not seriously injured. So Rockne turned his attention to the culprit who delivered the kind of debilitating hit normally reserved for Saturdays at the stadium. Krause had already slinked off the field, certain he had incurred Rockne's wrath this time. Instead, he had made a lasting impression on the coach. "That's the way to play this game," Rockne said. "I think you're going to make it at Notre Dame."

Rockne reaffirmed his prediction publicly at a postseason banquet. Celebrating an undefeated season and the 1930 national championship, Rockne could not resist a glimpse toward a future when Krause's physical prowess would be used against opposing players instead of his own. He promised his hulking freshman tackle would have a spot in the starting lineup. That news did not surprise anyone who had seen Krause on the practice field, but to the best of anybody's recollection, Rockne had never bestowed such praise on a rookie. "The older guys told me that was the first time they ever heard Rockne compliment a freshman," Krause said years later in a *Notre Dame Magazine* profile. "Well, I just about fell out of my chair."

Krause's respect and affection for Rockne became frozen in time on March 31, 1931. A plane crash in Kansas killed the coach, transforming an already larger-than-life figure into a legend and a symbol of the university he made famous from West Point to Hollywood. At home in Chicago for the Easter holiday when he heard the news, Krause "cried like a baby." He immediately returned to campus for the funeral. Sacred Heart Church overflowed with mourners as the university president Rev. Charles L. O'Donnell, trying to define Rockne's life, established his legend in death.

> What was the secret of his irresistible appeal to all sorts and conditions of men? Who shall pluck out the heart of his mystery and lay bare the inner source of the power he had? When we say simply, he was a great American, we shall go far towards satisfying many, for all of us recognize and love

the attributes of the true American character. When we say that he was an inspirer of young men in the direction of high ideals that were conspicuously exemplified in his own life, we have covered much that unquestionably was true of him. When we link his name to the intrinsic chivalry and romance of a great college game, which he, perhaps more than any other one man, has made finer and cleaner in itself and larger in its popular appeal, here, too, we touch upon a vital point. But no one of these things, nor all of them together can quite sum up this man whose tragic death at the early age of forty-three has left the country aghast. . . .

In an age that has stamped itself as the era of the "go-getter"—a horrible word for what is all-too-often a ruthless thing—he was a "go-giver"—a not much better word, but it means a divine thing. He made use of all the proper machinery and the legitimate methods of modern activity to be essentially not modern at all: to be quite elementarily human and Christian, giving himself, spending himself like water, not for himself, but for others. And once again, in his case, most illustriously is verified the Christian paradox—he has cast away to keep, he has lost his life to find it. This is not death but immortality.

Like the lecture Rockne had given him a few months earlier, Krause absorbed O'Donnell's words like a sponge, the thesis becoming a driving force in his professional life. He probably could not have articulated his feelings as a freshman who cowered and swooned in Rockne's presence, but Krause undoubtedly viewed his coach exactly as O'Donnell described him. As that idealized image took root and grew, it inspired Krause more than Rockne himself ever could have in their brief acquaintance.

✦ ✦ ✦

In Rockne's rollicking tenure spanning the Roaring Twenties, perhaps only Babe Ruth and Jack Dempsey had stirred the nation's sporting imagination more. Replacing him would be a monumental task. Like the stock market, Notre Dame's football fortunes had reached unprecedented levels. And, like the stock market, they would go into a steep, sudden decline.

Instead of one of Rockne's former players coaching in college who were rumored to replace him, Notre Dame named Rockne's top assistant Hunk Anderson "senior coach" and another lieutenant Jack Chevigny "junior coach." It was an awkward decision meant to avoid a prolonged search with spring practice approaching. "An obvious stopgap," Francis Wallace writes in *Notre Dame: From Rockne to Parseghian.* "It was all very sentimental and romantic, and was accepted by most as a fairly safe gamble."

O'Donnell asked Rockne's predecessor Jess Harper to leave the farm where he had retired in Kansas to assist Notre Dame in the transition by becoming athletic director. That job always had belonged to the football coach in the past. To ease the burden on Anderson and ensure the administration controlled the football program, O'Donnell inserted Harper into the chain of command.

O'Donnell and Vice President Rev. Michael Mulcaire instructed Harper to rein in Rockne's excesses in terms of scholarships and jobs doled out to football players. "O'Donnell and Mulcaire never wanted to have another athletic director/coach as autonomous and uncontrollable as he had been at Notre Dame," Robert Burns writes in *Being Catholic, Being American: The Notre Dame Story, 1842–1934.* "That was the new order of things."

Anderson protested to Harper, who told him to take it up with the bosses. Any athletic director not named Rockne would answer to O'Donnell and Mulcaire. Harper said he was just doing their bidding.

According to Anderson's memoir, he told O'Donnell, "If you starve the goose, it will stop laying the golden egg."

"The goose has been overfed," O'Donnell said, "and while it is digesting the feed, it will continue to lay the golden egg."

Anderson's tenure as "senior coach" began successfully enough in 1931. He won six of his first seven games and played to a scoreless tie with Northwestern on the strength of a dominant line Krause anchored. In a slow-moving slog through the mud, Krause recovered a blocked punt at the Wildcats' 19-yard line in one of the game's few memorable moments.

Penciled in as a second-string tackle his sophomore season, Krause stepped in after a recurring knee injury sidelined starter Al Culver. Krause seldom left the field again. Anderson may have lacked many of Rockne's most beloved and respected characteristics, but he could coach linemen, and Krause flourished under his direction. Intense and intimidating, Krause could punish opponents with his power or fool them with his footwork. With Krause rooted at left tackle and established star Joe Kurth on the right side, only Pittsburgh, USC and Army scored against the Irish in a 6-2-1 season.

After the sixth game against Navy in Baltimore, O'Donnell announced the coaching arrangement with Anderson and Chevigny would be permanent. Despite Notre Dame's success, the decision surprised observers who expected an individual replacement for Rockne to be named, presumably from among the several experienced head coaches who had played for him. Anderson himself apparently expected that. "He was as perplexed about his role as everyone else," longtime *South Bend Tribune* sports editor Joe Doyle writes in *A Century of Notre Dame Football.* Even as he won games, he failed to win over fans. That may have been inevitable under the circumstances. Rockne's sterling record and captivating personality had become the standard Notre Dame fans expected, magnifying Anderson's every misstep.

When the Irish faced USC in the first-ever sellout at Notre Dame Stadium one week after the announcement about the coaching situation, a twenty-six-game unbeaten streak dating back to 1929 ended. Anderson made questionable substitutions that allowed USC to claw back from a two-touchdown deficit to win 16-14. Rules prohibited players from returning in the same quarter when they were replaced and the absence of some starters, including Krause, helped ignite the Trojan rally.

After a loss to Army the next week in the season finale, Anderson articulated the concern that seemed to nag fans all year. "Perhaps," he said, "only Rockne could have pulled our team out of the doldrums for that game."

✦ ✦ ✦

Krause stepped into a more stable situation with the Notre Dame basketball program. George Keogan had been the coach since 1923 and built the Irish into national champions in 1926 and '27, winning thirty-eight games and losing only two in that span. In the ensuing three seasons, Notre Dame lacked a dominant offensive force, a problem solved when Krause first laced his sneakers as a sophomore. He played sparingly for the first few games as he built his stamina after football ended and the Irish staggered to a 3-2 start. They would not lose again, with his creative presence occupying most of the space beneath the basket. "He had the ability to clown and play at the same time," McAloon says. "He would waltz dribbling the ball and be bowing to the people, a big laugh on his face, everyone roaring with laughter."

Krause's performances, as spectacular as they were playful, made him a favorite of the frenzied students who filled the Notre Dame Fieldhouse for every game. He also gave the *South Bend Tribune* a repetitive storyline as the Irish stormed to an 18-2 record behind his scoring prowess and passing finesse:

KRAUSE LEADS
ATTACK WITH
SEVEN GOALS

"Krause, whose specialty was football until last night, sank seven goals from the field and three free throws for 17 points to take individual scoring honors. In addition he was a tower of strength on defense. His work under the basket was phenomenal and several times he broke up Marquette drives down the court by intercepting passes."

FAST PASSES
FEATURE TENTH
WIN FOR IRISH

"Ed Krause handled the pivot job in expert fashion and the passes he worked with Ray DeCook absolutely baffled Iowa's guards."

KRAUSE STARS
AS IRISH WIN
NINTH IN ROW

"Ed 'Moose' Krause, giant gridiron star . . . possessed an unerring eye for the hoop, registering from the foul line eight times, which with a field goal, gave him a total of 10 points. The speedy Notre Dame passing attack centered about Krause to-night and it clicked to perfection."

KRAUSE STARS
IN 32-25 WIN
AT CLEVELAND

"The Irish attack was led by Krause, the smoothest college basketball player to show in Cleveland this year. Not one of Krause's shots traveled more than a half dozen feet. He simply stationed himself under the basket and acted as pivot of Notre Dame's attack."

Krause led the Irish to sixteen straight wins and "firmly established himself as . . . one of the premier pivotmen in at least the Midwest," Tim Neely writes in *Hooping It Up: The Complete History of Notre Dame Basketball.* "Krause's contribution to the Irish surge was recognized by several All-

American selection committees, making him the first ND sophomore to receive such honors."

✦ ✦ ✦

No matter how many honors he accumulated on the basketball court, Krause would always be considered a football player first at Notre Dame. No matter how much his personality and choreography shone through on the Fieldhouse floor, it would be obscured by his sheer power in a gridiron scrum. No matter how dramatically his presence altered the balance of power under the basket, he remained grass-stained and bruised from the physical ferocity of football until the (increasingly bitter) end. Toiling in relative obscurity along the offensive and defensive lines meant more at Notre Dame than being the basketball team's literal center of attention.

As the 1932 season began, the football program seemed more than two years removed from the Rockne era. Something fundamental had changed, a shift evident in the two losses that ended the previous year and magnified throughout another season that seemed modestly successful on the surface, but lacked the vibrant spirit of the past. Journalist and author Francis Wallace writes that Notre Dame's role had changed in the college football hierarchy from the hero of the season's greatest upsets to the victim. "Under Hunk," Wallace says, "Notre Dame was learning to lose."

Again the beneficiary of great line play, Anderson's specialty, Notre Dame lost only to eventual Rose Bowl opponents Pittsburgh and USC in 1932. "Our line held the other seven opponents scoreless," Anderson writes in his memoir. "Joe Kurth and Ed 'Moose' Krause were our tackles and possibly the best two tackles I have ever coached." They opened holes on offense and clogged them on defense, a particularly perilous job description considering the relatively sparse padding they wore.

Without facemasks on their leather helmets, they often left the field with noses bloodied or broken to accompany the bruises tenderizing the rest of their bodies. They embodied Anderson's toughness and hardened approached to football and life.

What Anderson did not have was the creativity and charisma that distinguished Rockne from his peers. It may have been unfair to expect it, but among spoiled Notre Dame fans, two losses for the second straight season only increased the volume of the criticism. "Almost as soon as the 1932 season was completed," Anderson said, "rumor got back to me that my days were numbered at Notre Dame."

✦ ✦ ✦

All the controversy engulfing Anderson and the football program made the continuity and consistency Keogan had established in basketball all the more remarkable. Keogan never approached Rockne's legendary status, but he built a respected program and inspired a student following so loyal and loud, opponents feared the Fieldhouse itself as much as any Irish player. His status on campus insulated him somewhat from criticism during a mediocre start to the 1932–33 season.

Keogan also had to contend with a new rule designed to diminish the dominance of Krause and other muscular, immovable men in the middle. To prevent powerful "pivot" players from controlling play under the basket, a "three-second violation" became a part of the basketball lexicon. It required anyone in possession of the ball inside the free throw lane to pass or shoot within three seconds.

"This rule removes from basketball one of the best scoring plays and a maneuver that has been in the game since before the days of the old National Professional League," the *South Bend Tribune* reported in a 1932 explanatory article about the change. "It takes away the premium of the large and sturdy player who was clever at handling the ball and keeping it away from adversaries by swinging the sphere from side to side."

Krause had been as adept at that maneuver as any player in the country the previous season, pivoting his opponents into dizziness with the ball indefinitely in his hands. Now he would have to make quicker decisions, his size less of a premium than his swift footwork and quick thinking. Also, as the *South Bend Tribune* article explained, the rule applied only if a player had both feet in the lane. Straddling the line would not invoke the violation, allowing Krause and other pivot men to continue their cunning maneuvers just a few steps farther from the basket.

As Krause worked himself into basketball shape, he fouled out of a loss to Marquette and hit just two of eleven field-goal attempts in a loss to Michigan State. He steadied himself to score 12 points against Pittsburgh, but the Irish lost again, falling to 6-6. With frustration festering, they stopped in Toledo to stretch their legs with a game on the way back from Pittsburgh. A winning streak that would last 364 days began with a 42-14 thumping of the University of Toledo, though the trip itself ended less successfully.

Feeling generous after the big win, Keogan gave the players a few hours of freedom before catching the train back to South Bend. He insisted they arrive an hour before the scheduled departure, at eleven o'clock. Keogan made Krause responsible for seeing that they were on time. Busy entertaining the girls of Toledo, they lost track of time and had to hustle to hop aboard the eleven o'clock train as it pulled out of the station. Just catching their breath as the conductor came around asking for tickets, they informed him their coach had them. "What coach?" the conductor said. Keogan wanted the team to gather at the station at eleven o'clock for the midnight train out of Toledo. Krause and his teammates had misunderstood. So while Keogan waited for his players to arrive at the station, they were already chugging toward South Bend. Without tickets, of course, they could not get that far. Escorted off the train at Elkhart, about twenty miles east of South Bend, they waited at the local police station for Keogan, never the most understanding fellow, to arrive and vouch for them. It may have been the only time in history a team has had to run laps as a punishment for being early.

Adventures on the road defined the 1932–33 team, which finished with a modest 16-6 record, but made their trips memorable. Down in Indianapolis in the midst of their season-ending winning streak, the Irish appeared on the verge of defeat in the closing seconds against Butler. True to their nickname, the Bulldogs protected their home court with a snarling tenacity. Notre Dame eagerly joined the fray. So often a showman on the court, Krause also relished the rebounding battles that required him to throw his weight around.

With Butler protecting a two-point lead, Krause missed a potential tying shot with time running out. Bodies collided and crashed to the Hinkle Fieldhouse floor in the battle for the precious rebound. "In this wild rush I was either pushed or tripped, or else fell from exhaustion," Krause said. "At any rate, there I was stretched out on the hardwood with players jumping on and off my head as fast as I could count." Sprawled flat on his back, Krause saw only the soles of sneakers dangerously close to his face until his own missed shot bounced right back into his arms. "Without moving," Notre Dame's campus weekly *The Scholastic* reported, "he shot the ball from his prostrate position and tied the score."

Notre Dame needed more magic in overtime. Jim Newbold, who rarely played, tipped in the game-winning basket for a frenetic 42-41 win. Keogan praised Krause afterward for the resilience he displayed in even attempting that supine shot, his will to win still evident when many others would have given up. As Krause relates the story, he was acting more out of self-preservation than persistence. He tossed the ball away like a hot potato, "in the general direction of the basket." Keogan also teased him a bit to make sure Krause's opinion of himself did not inflate.

"You ought to keep shooting them from a horizontal position, Ed," Keogan said. "You're more accurate that way than on your feet."

Though he knew his shot was the result of dumb luck more than determination, Krause played the role of hero with his usual aplomb. Walking out of the hotel the next morning, the Irish encountered a kid hawking copies of the *Indianapolis Star*.

"Morning Star!"

"Good morning, young man," Krause said, patting him on the head.

All the Irish would get in on the joke at practice that afternoon. To prove to Keogan that they all possessed Krause's resolute spirit, they concluded their warm-ups with a new drill. Keogan walked on the court to discover his players lying flat on the floor and basketballs bouncing wildly from their attempts to recreate the previous night's drama.

His joke with the newspaper boy notwithstanding, Krause quickly was becoming a star. Two All-American basketball seasons along with his impressive notices on the most prominent football team in the nation had made him a well-known figure from Yankee Stadium to the Los Angeles Coliseum. For all his accolades, he remained humble, even self-effacing, becoming as popular on campus as he was powerful on the field.

Krause did not smoke or drink, in part because he had to stay in shape, and in part because Notre Dame students generally lived sheltered lives. "A big night back then," 1933 graduate and future chairman of the university board of trustees Edmund Stephan says, "was to have a milkshake or a black cow and head down to the Colfax Theatre to see Clara Bow."

Krause studied journalism, but felt a pull toward the priesthood, his inherently religious nature unchanged by his taste of material success and the professional opportunities available to star athletes. While his essential character remained steadfast, a senior year of triumph and tragedy, of disappointment and discovery, would alter the course of Krause's life.

✦ ✦ ✦

Rev. John "Pop" Farley, the colorful rector of Sorin Hall and former Notre Dame football player, disconnected the electronic bell system that rang across campus and rousted his students with his own cowbell. If they failed to stir fast enough, he would open their door and hit them with it until they didn't know if the ringing was from the bell or in their heads.

Even the daily mail call became an anxious ordeal on Pop Farley's watch. He collected all the letters and stood at the top of the stairs, calling out names and offering a running commentary on their correspondence. "McCormick, it's a girl writing to you. I can smell it. Now Mac, I'm going to hold this letter for a day because your grades are going down. You're reading too damn many letters. Now, raise your grades and I'll give it to you."

Sorin Hall had a reputation as a sedate environment, "a very solid, staid old man," as the Notre Dame yearbook described it. Yet like Pop Farley himself, whose thinning gray hair and wire-rimmed glasses suggested a demure demeanor, Sorin Hall had a boisterous heart beneath the surface.

Sorin's resident prefect of discipline, Father DeReimus, often went down to the campus lakes and captured ducks. He cooked them in his room, adding a pleasant aroma to dorm life. Rev. John O'Hara, a future president of Notre Dame, lived in Sorin's "Tower Room." He produced a daily religious bulletin with the exploits of a fictional know-it-all student named Cardinal McGutskey, who represented the hubris of the young men on campus. O'Hara's bulletin prodded them, in its humorous way, to become better Christian gentlemen. He also offered a sympathetic ear every night for any students to vent their problems or complaints, as sacrosanct as a confessional. "It was known as the gripe tower," McAloon says. "You could go in and let go . . . it was between you and he."

Nothing caused more griping on campus that fall than the foibles of the Notre Dame football team. Hunk Anderson called the 1933 season "the year that the seeds of deemphasis were harvested into a disappointing crop." Disappointment does not begin to describe the reaction to a 3-5-1 record that made Anderson a man under siege. He endured criticism and second-guessing from fans across the country during a four-game streak when Notre Dame failed to score. Newspapers reported rumors of an imminent dismissal. An Associated Press report dubbed Anderson "the haunted man."

As the 1933 Irish spiraled toward the first losing record since Notre Dame's 1-2 mark in 1888, even the most loyal audience reacted with disgust. "Sadly lacking the traditional Irish blocking, spirit and fight, Notre Dame went down to a 7-0 defeat at the hands of Carnegie Tech," *The Scholastic* informed the student body. Francis Wallace said it was a team that was "brave enough but not smart enough, that was eager but uncertain, anxious but ineffective, that was playing with body and emotion but lacking that mental and spiritual edge that had been its trademark in the past."

Anderson had instituted a policy of naming different captains for each game, a plan the *South Bend Tribune* criticized for creating a leadership vacuum that contributed to the inconsistent performances. Loyal sons of Notre Dame like Hugh Devore and Moose Krause led the team each in their turn, but passing the buck from week to week never required anyone to bear responsibility. Naming different captains almost encouraged players to dismiss it as an honorary title with little more to be concerned about than calling heads or tails at the coin toss.

Krause endured a personal loss that made all the press criticism and alumni anger seem insignificant. When Walter Krauciunas opened the butcher shop one morning, a robber held him up at gunpoint, killing Krause's father before fleeing without a trace. Krause seldom discussed it and never divulged any details about the incident or how it affected him, other than how it redirected his professional ambitions.

It ended his thoughts of becoming a priest because he would have to earn a steady income to help his widowed mother. It also may have been the moment when how he played the game became more important to him than winning or losing. For the first time, Krause had experienced a true, lasting loss. From that moment on, games would be just that—important in their place, but certainly not life and death. Krause never explicitly articulated those feelings. His actions in the aftermath of his father's death suggested an increased commitment to the ideal of pursuing victory with honor and keeping sports in proper perspective.

When Southern California visited Notre Dame in late November, Krause took it upon himself to seek out the Trojans' star running back Cotton Warburton. A broken nose earlier in the season required Warburton to wear a bulky protective mask he hated. Opponents aimed cheap shots at his injured snout, their best defense against the small but shifty USC back. Krause told Warburton he would not have to wear the mask against the Irish. He assured him the Notre Dame players would not stoop to that level. Warburton probably did not need the sportsmanlike concession from Krause. Broken nose or not, he carried the ball 19 times for 95 yards and two touchdowns in the Trojans' 19-0 rout.

Krause shook Warburton's hand afterward, disappointed in another defeat, but finding solace in the prayer attributed to Rockne about the value of honest competition.

Dear Lord,
In the battle that goes on for life,
I ask for a field that is fair,
A chance that is equal with all in strife,
The courage to do and to dare.

If I should win, let it be by the code,
My faith and my honor held high.
If I should lose, let me stand by the road,
And cheer as the winner rides by.

A week later against Army at Yankee Stadium, a tenacious Krause again fought the good fight against an overpowering opponent with another loss apparently inevitable. Notre Dame's season appeared destined to end in appropriately gloomy fashion against the undefeated Cadets, who led 12-0 with five minutes to play. It could have been worse, but Army missed both its point-after attempts, including one Krause blocked.

Anderson sensed "desperation turning into fury," as Nick Lukats scored a touchdown to make the score 12-7. "Vicious line play" then stopped the Cadets deep in their own territory, forcing them to punt. Concerned about another Krause block, Army linemen cheated to his side. He even took a couple of steps toward the sideline to draw them farther from the center of the line. "This was a set up for the Army forwards," *The Scholastic* reported. "They blocked out Krause but in doing so they forgot all about (Wayne) Millner who rushed in almost unmolested, leaped high into the air and blocked the punt with his chest. The ball bounced in the end zone. Millner was after it like a scared rabbit. He fell on it" for the winning touchdown.

The Scholastic captured the moment in breathless prose that seemed to ring with the words of the Victory March, "what though the odds be great or small, old Notre Dame will win over all!"

Notre Dame came back Saturday.

Notre Dame came back from the oblivion of a record marred with five defeats and from the depths of a score which stood 12 to 0 against them at the end of the third quarter to overwhelm a previously undefeated Army team, 13-12. Came back with an attack which for pure fury and force has never been surpassed. Came back to score more points in five dramatic minutes of the last quarter than they had in any previous game.

All the pent-up and undelivered power of the Irish was released in that hectic final quarter. Notre Dame's line, which just a week before had been ripped to shreds by Southern California's forwards, shoved aside and completely outmaneuvered the vaunted Army linemen.

✦ ✦ ✦

Krause's final football game left a good taste in his mouth after a bitter season, but he had little time to savor it. One of Notre Dame's best basketball seasons ever was taking shape, and he hustled over to the Fieldhouse to take his place at the center of it. After winning their final eleven games in Krause's junior season, the Irish extended their streak to twenty-two at the start of the 1933–34 season. With four starters back and a talented complement of sophomores, Notre Dame beat Purdue for the first time, defeated Northwestern twice and survived a tense, physical three-overtime wrestling match at Michigan State, 34-33. A talented Marquette team also threatened the streak, but Krause's 11 points led the Irish to a 30-28 edge.

On a trip to Pittsburgh, where Notre Dame had last lost a basketball game 364 days before, the streak ended. Ahead 27-16 midway through the second half, the Irish could not maintain the emotion they displayed in building the lead. Pittsburgh raced back to win, 39-34.

A new streak reached six wins with relative ease, including one of the most impressive individual performances in Notre Dame history. "The showman," Tim Neely writes in *Hooping It Up*, "was the amazing Edward 'Moose' Krause." On February 6, just four days after his twenty-first birthday, Krause celebrated at the Fieldhouse with 22 points in a win over Minnesota, the most points for an Irish player in a decade.

Notre Dame stood at 17-1 with a chance to avenge its only loss when Pittsburgh visited the Fieldhouse for a rematch on February 17.

They gave the overflow crowd little to cheer in a defensive struggle that finished with a football score. Pittsburgh held Krause to just two points, negating Notre Dame's own suffocating defense and handing the Irish their second defeat, 21-17.

Two more wins set the stage for an emotional home finale against Ohio State. Voegele scored 12 points and Krause added 10 as they basked in the enthusiastic appreciation of the crowd. For the first time in the Keogan era, and only the second time in history, Notre Dame had won twenty games.

They would not add to that total. Two road games to end the season provided a disappointing denouement to Krause's basketball career and cost the Irish any chance for a national championship. Marquette and Minnesota, which had each lost to Notre Dame earlier in the season, took distinctly different approaches to defending Krause with identical results.

Marquette deluged him with double teams. They shadowed his every step, as many other teams had tried, but this time the rest of the team failed to take advantage of their increased opportunities and the Irish lost 21-20. Minnesota, meanwhile, gave Krause ample room to maneuver while clamping down on the rest of the Irish. He scored 14 points in his final college game and Leo Crowe added 11, but their teammates contributed only 16 more in a 43-41 overtime loss.

✦ ✦ ✦

Krause spent his final few months in college in the usual social pursuits. He served as chairman of the music committee for the annual Monogram Club dance and organized two hundred of his closest friends to attend a sorority dance in downtown South Bend. With the promise of free food and drink, not to mention two hundred women with empty dance cards, Krause's powers of persuasion were not challenged.

He met a woman at the dance named Elizabeth Linden, who also grew up on the south side of Chicago, about forty blocks south of Krause's old neighborhood. She had a luminous smile and a confidence in the way she carried herself that drew Krause to her.

He told Elizabeth he would be in Chicago for the summer and asked her for a date. She said no. A serious suitor, her fiancé in fact, awaited back home. True to the ideals he had learned on the football field, Krause refused to give up "what though the odds." Elizabeth fended off his persistent queries with the deftness of an opposing lineman, but he would continue to pursue her.

Krause had other opportunities to find female companionship. Keogan took him to a YMCA banquet after his senior season, introducing him to several women in attendance. Keogan offered Krause a cigar for the occasion, which he smoked and held between his fingers like a connoisseur. It felt comfortable and people complimented him for his taste. His confidence swelled and he proposed a toast before the assembled crowd. "Here's to the ladies," Krause said. "The best years of my life I've spent with another man's wife—my mother."

"Hey," a surprised Keogan said, "that's pretty good."

"After that," Krause said, "I kept on smoking."

On the steps of Sorin Hall days before his graduation, Krause received an award that exceeded all his sporting laurels. He had made such an impression on the student body as an athlete and a gentleman that they honored him with a trophy. "It was an extemporaneous idea, stemming from his classmates and participated in by the student body," longtime Notre Dame sports information director Charlie Callahan said. Rev.

O'Hara made the presentation to Krause, who remains the only Notre Dame student ever to receive such an honor.

A few months after graduating cum laude with a degree in journalism and just weeks before starting his first job as athletic director and coach of all sports at Saint Mary's College in Winona, Minnesota, Krause played one last football game. Fans selected a college all-star team to face the professional champion Chicago Bears in an exhibition at Soldier Field. "I don't even know how I got on the team," Krause said, "except my friends from the Back of the Yards probably voted four or five times, as usual."

Krause already had turned down a lucrative offer from George Halas to play for the Bears because of the young league's roughneck reputation. On August 21, 1934, he discovered he had made a good decision. Fierce, snarling linemen like George Musso put up enough of a fight against a collection of college kids who practiced together for only a few days before the game. And the elusive Red Grange lived up to his nickname as "The Galloping Ghost," disappearing before defenders could wrap him up, though Krause boasted that he tackled him. "Once," Krause said.

Bronko Nagurski was the real beast, a running back so powerful that Musso warned Krause across the line of scrimmage that he would be running in their direction.

"What do you want me to do about it?" Krause said.

"I don't know," Musso said, "but I'm getting the hell out of his way."

Krause collided with Nagurski and the rest of the Bears a little too often, as a newspaper photo vividly showed a day after the scoreless draw. Resting in a hospital bed, Krause smiled for the camera, but his crooked, swollen nose and puffy eyes revealed the damage the professional game could do. Pursuing less hazardous employment felt like a wise choice.

The Midnight Rides of Moose Krause

KRAUSE'S ATHLETIC REPUTATION, AND HIS CONNEC-
tion to the Christian Brothers who ran DeLaSalle
High, earned him a job at a time when many of his
Notre Dame classmates struggled to find work. He turned down $425 a
game from George Halas to play for the Chicago Bears, choosing instead
a $2,500-a-year offer from the Christian Brothers to be athletic director
and coach of all sports at Saint Mary's College in Winona, Minnesota.

Brother Julius Hughes, who had been transferred to Saint Mary's
after fifteen years at DeLaSalle, wrote to Krause during his senior year
to gauge his interest. "Are you going to coach next year? And if so, have
you something fixed in your mind? If you have not, and you desire to
coach, would you desire to come here? . . . It would be a great pleasure
for me to have a Brother's boy here."

Krause arrived in the fall of 1934 at the sleepy campus called Terrace
Heights, with a view of the bluffs along the Mississippi River banks, to

guide an athletic program in its infancy. In addition to his duties as athletic director and coach of all sports, his contract called for him to head
the journalism and physical education departments in exchange for his
modest salary, room, board and laundry service.

From a student body of 300, only fourteen young men went out for
football. None weighed more than 150 pounds. Their hulking mentor
weighed in at a muscular 240, his stature made larger by his famous
football pedigree. Krause took it easy on the Redmen, backing off during blocking drills for fear of injuring them. His inspirational speeches
lacked the magnetic intensity of Rockne, his lifelong model for all things
athletic. "[Krause's] rhetoric wasn't as good as Rock's," Stephen Singular
writes in *Notre Dame's Greatest Coaches*, "and neither were his teams,
which were regularly trounced." With a little more raw material, Krause
built the Saint Mary's basketball program into something resembling
respectability, once winning a conference championship. He also
coached the baseball, track, golf and tennis teams.

Krause understood Saint Mary's would never be Notre Dame.
Competitive by nature, he coveted winning but knew better than to
obsess about it at a small, obscure school where fielding a team represented a victory in itself. As one contemporary profile of Krause noted,
indirectly indicting the state of Redmen athletics, "No man is too small,
too clumsy or too green to merit Ed's attention to his development if
the man is willing to try."

Krause meant much more to Saint Mary's than wins and losses. His
presence gave the school a certain athletic validation, and a higher profile than it could have otherwise achieved. Krause's star continued to rise
on the court, which only enhanced his reputation off of it. He formed
a barnstorming semi-pro basketball team, playing on weekends from
Kalamazoo to Oshkosh to Sioux City, supplementing his income with
$35 a game and a share of the gate receipts, a star's ransom. He made
the papers all over the Midwest, his presence usually assuring a healthy

crowd—and paycheck—that made all the travel worthwhile. Saint Mary's played its basketball games on Friday nights, so Krause and his teammates would hop a midnight train to anyplace they could find an opponent. Often they returned to Winona early on Monday mornings, just in time to begin a new work week.

"KRAUSE IS BRILLIANT" blared one headline after his team defeated the Harlem Globetrotters, a frequent opponent, in an exhibition in Sioux Falls, South Dakota, in 1935. "As quick as a cat when he flew into action on post plays under the basket despite his 240 pounds," according to one account, Krause scored 12 points to lead his "makeshift basketball team" to victory. They played a rematch the next night in Mitchell, South Dakota, with Krause again leading his team with 15 points, but the Globetrotters flashy athleticism won out this time in a 41-34 win.

Even in the north, the Globetrotters faced racial segregation and discrimination. They endured derisive newspaper descriptions like "eight balls" and "black aces." One promoter tried to cheat team owner Abe Saperstein out of the share of the money he had been promised, offering the balance to Krause, who angrily told the promoter to give the Globetrotters their due. Saperstein overheard the conversation, forging a lifelong friendship. "My father always said the Globetrotters could not have had any kind of success without the support of guys like Moose Krause," says Jerry Saperstein, the son of Globetrotters founder. "He always considered Moose Krause one of his heroes, really, because he was a guy who was there when there wasn't anybody else, an early, early supporter of the Globetrotters when they had damn few others."

"I got to know the Globetrotters like my brothers," Krause says in *Notre Dame's Greatest Coaches*. "We played against them in Sioux Falls, South Dakota, and in Wisconsin and Michigan and North Dakota. They couldn't sleep in the hotels in these places and had to sleep in their cars. Sometimes we snuck them into our rooms after the games and they were able to sleep there."

Krause's salary was sufficient, even substantial for the time, especially with his basketball moonlighting. But with his mother forced to work in the stockyards after her husband's death, Krause regularly sent money home to help. He also spent his summers in Chicago, working odd jobs to make ends meet. Filling in for vacationing milkmen and selling sprinklers to local Catholic parishes, Krause made a little extra money for himself and his mother.

Whatever he had leftover he spent courting Elizabeth Linden. Krause's persistent pursuit since they met at the sorority dance in South Bend finally succeeded. They spent as much time as possible together during Krause's summers in Chicago in the mid-1930s, though both had the details of their own lives to occupy them. Elise (pronounced A-lis), as her friends called her, had worked as a secretary at First National Bank of Chicago since her graduation from the Catholic, all-girls Visitation High School on 57th Street, not far from the Back of the Yards. She grew up among the Germans and "lace-curtain Irish," living relatively comfortably on her father's salary as an electrical engineer. "We never knew there was a Depression," Elise's brother, Joe Linden, says. "Our father had a good, steady income, an automobile, a nice place to live."

Elise's exuberant personality dominated most situations. Her beaming smile exuded charm and charisma. Always style-conscious and popular among her peers, Elise had been the basketball team captain at Visitation, not the star player but unquestionably the leader.

Though Elise's engagement to "some Irishman," as Krause referred to him in *Notre Dame's Greatest Coaches*, had foiled his early requests for dates, her engaging personality, bright smile and lithe, athletic frame inspired him to keep trying. Her engagement eventually ended for reasons apparently forgotten at that fork in the road, one loss for the Irish that never bothered Krause.

Ed and Elise fell in love long distance, no small challenge during the days of economic stagnation, overnight train rides and primarily handwritten communication. Elise and her sister, Dorothy, traveled to Winona one weekend a month to visit Ed. He passed through Chicago on basketball trips and spent his summers at home, but that would be their only personal contact during a four-year courtship.

✦ ✦ ✦

In the summer of 1935, Ed and Phil Krause and a group of other Lithuanian-American athletes from Chicago traveled to Kaunas, Lithuania, as emissaries of sports. Accepting an invitation from the government, eleven athletes spent three weeks giving the novice Lithuanians demonstrations and lessons in basketball, track, boxing, swimming and volleyball. Leaders of Chicago's Lithuanian community spent months raising money for the three-week journey and selecting the members of what would be dubbed the "Lithuanian-American Olympic Team." Chicago's teeming Lithuanian population championed their cause, contributing whatever they could, and jamming the LaSalle Street Station for a boisterous sendoff on July 30, 1935. "The boys had tears in their eyes as the train pulled out," Krause wrote in an essay about his experience.

Poignantly noting the Statue of Liberty and Ellis Island as they churned out of New York Harbor, these children of immigrants traveled to Europe in style aboard the *Normandie*, "the largest and most luxurious liner afloat." Wearing blue blazers emblazoned with the Lithuanian and American flags and crisp white slacks the fundraisers helped provide, they basked in the opulence for more than four days en route to their first stop in France. "We participated in deck-tennis, shuffle board, ping pong, swimming, boxing and wrestling which kept us quite busy," Krause wrote. "In the evenings dancing was the sport which attracted the attention of the boys. Besides all these activities there were three meals a day which the athletes ate to their hearts' content."

For one night in Paris, their hearts would not be content with food. In search of more decadent diversions, the evening "was enjoyed by all except our manager and coach who ran around all night getting the boys to bed, fearing that they might get lost in this town of midnight prowlings."

It took three days and nights aboard trains from France, through Belgium and Germany, to reach the Lithuanian border, where the foreign language most familiar to these thoroughly American athletes filled them with a sense of home. They cheered and hugged and sang patriotic songs as they crossed the border. "As long as I live," Krause wrote, "I never will again hear the Lithuanian Anthem sung with such feeling, with such fervor, and with such a tone of loyalty."

Feted like celebrities and peppered with questions from young Lithuanians about life in America, at times the group felt more like a diplomatic delegation than an athletic one. Their contribution to the sporting life of Lithuania would be instructive, inspirational and indelible.

Not long before their arrival, Lithuania had lost to Latvia in the 1935 European basketball championships, 131-10. Spurred by this brief encounter with American athletes and the coaching of Krause's brother, Phil, who stayed in the country for four years to teach the game, the Lithuanians won the European championship in 1937. Two years later, they hosted the tournament in Kaunas and repeated their remarkable feat in front of their home fans.

Soon Nazi tanks started rolling, Phil Krause fled back to the States and darkness enveloped the continent. A world war and Communist aggression altered the balance of power in the world and on European scoreboards. Before any of these loyal Lithuanian-Americans could return, Soviet occupation closed an iron curtain over its once welcoming borders. As the Cold War drove an ideological wedge between East and West, an image haunted the Americans who made that journey in the summer of 1935, a vivid vision of their goodwill violently turned against them: Lithuanian athletes wearing the uniform of the USSR.

✦ ✦ ✦

Back in Winona, Krause tried to build Saint Mary's athletic program using Rockne's template, challenging the best teams he could and never shying away from a publicity gimmick. He agreed to participate in a college-football first on November 16, 1934—an indoor game. Traveling to Chicago for this "home game," Saint Mary's faced Saint Viator of Bourbonnais, Illinois, at the Field Artillery Armory at 52nd Street and Cottage Grove Avenue. On a clay field two yards short at the end lines, but otherwise conforming to regulations, the teams entertained a capacity crowd of 7,000 in the stale air. Saint Mary's lost, 7-0, but gained increased press attention, invaluable currency for a growing program. Although the stunt did not "revolutionize the game of football," as one newspaper account suggested it might, it did earn the Redmen more column inches than a traditional game would have.

Preparing his basketball schedule in similar publicity-conscious fashion, Krause called his old Notre Dame coach, George Keogan, seeking exposure for his team with a game in the Fieldhouse he once dominated. Keogan agreed to play the Redmen on a Saturday in December 1935. Krause excitedly informed Saint Mary's athletic council chairman, Brother Matthew, of this high-profile addition to the schedule. Brother Matthew told Krause the team could not make the trip. An annual school retreat began the day after the game would be played, and the train ride back from South Bend would force the basketball players to miss the mandatory gathering. That would not be permitted. Krause often tried to lobby Brother Matthew—also known as "Brother Candy" because of his galloping sweet tooth—with a box of chocolates to advance the athletic department's interests. This decision, however, could not be swayed with sweets.

Krause mentioned the problem to a friend from Winona, Max Conrad, a passionate pilot and a former Notre Dame athlete. "Let's fly the team to South Bend," Conrad said. "We can . . . get them back in plenty of time for the retreat." Using Conrad's six-seater and another plane donated and flown by a friend, the team made it to South Bend and to the retreat, apparently the first time a college team had traveled together by air. Saint Mary's lost the game 45-22, "but the kids looked upon it as a great adventure," Krause said in a *St. Louis Globe-Democrat* story after Conrad's death in 1979. "They had a ball." Thinking back on the decision to fly, less than five years after Rockne's death in a plane crash, Krause shuddered at the risk they took. "Remember, this had never been done before. We had to get permission from the parents, which we did. But we had no insurance. It was (very) cold in the plane—but it all worked out."

Krause became a frequent flyer with Conrad. Like basketball, Saint Mary's also played its football games on Friday nights. That left Krause free on fall Saturdays to climb into Conrad's two-seater and fly to South Bend for Notre Dame football games. "He'd just put his plane down in some pasture," Krause said, "and we'd hitch a ride to the football field."

Krause put his journalism degree to work in the summer of 1937, writing a column for the *Town of Lake Journal*, a neighborhood newspaper in the Back of the Yards. He mused on a variety of sports issues of the era from the college football all-star game he helped inaugurate to the U.S. tour of the 1937 European champion Lithuanian basketball team.

> Town of Lake residents are doubly happy to learn of the arrival of these athletes, since the leader and coach of the basketball squad is my big brother, Phil, who lives at home, 4614 South Paulina. [Phil] has been in Lithuania for the past three months, coaching the Lithuanians and leading them to

the European championship in the tournament held in Riga, Latvia, where the Lithuanians defeated Italy, 23 to 21, in the final game.

To those who know anything about the athletic set-up in Lithuania, this feat seems an impossibility since their boys started to play basketball only two years ago.

In the true sportswriting tradition of the time, Krause served as a promoter as much as a reporter during his brief stint as a columnist. As if returning the favor bestowed on him three years earlier, Krause urged neighborhood residents to cast their all-star ballot for Mississippi State end Charlie Gelatka, a Back of the Yards boy. "I have known Charlie from his high school days on, and know that he deserves the honor of being on the All-Star team," Krause wrote. "I sincerely hope that everyone in the neighborhood will cast his vote for Chuck this week." An editor's note informed readers that they could aid Gelatka's cause with ballots available at the newspaper office.

Krause always displayed that kind of loyalty to his roots, either in his childhood neighborhood or at Notre Dame. A well-known and popular figure in the Back of the Yards and beyond, people often wanted him to be associated with their cause or to help sell their product. He almost always obliged.

Former Notre Dame tackle Frank Leahy, a rising star in the football coaching profession, worked with U.S. Rubber Corp. to develop canvas sneakers for basketball players. Leahy called Krause at Saint Mary's to ask him if he could attend a demonstration of the new shoes for a group of basketball coaches in Chicago. Krause checked his schedule and had to decline because a faculty meeting required him to be in Winona the night before.

"I decided that the only thing I could do would be to hire male models who might be able to impersonate basketball players," Leahy says in Wells Twombley's biography of the coach, *Shake Down the Thunder.* "Even then, male models did not look even vaguely like athletes." One thousand coaches would be in the auditorium for Leahy's demonstration. Watching the models' futile attempts to master the fundamentals of the game during a rehearsal, "I was in despair," he says. "As it came closer and closer to my nine A.M. demonstration, I decided that God simply didn't want Frank Leahy to succeed at this business venture."

At the last minute, Krause arrived after an overnight trip from Minnesota. He brought several other former players he had recruited from their beds that morning. An ecstatic Leahy proudly walked onto the stage, grabbed the microphone and said, "Gentlemen of the basketball coaching profession, it is my intense pleasure as a graduate of Notre Dame to present Ed Krause, who is probably the greatest basketball player Our Lady ever produced."

He made the shoes, and Leahy, look good. "That single act of loyalty," Leahy says, "saved my position with U.S. Rubber and enabled me to have some sort of financial latitude in my life when I desperately needed it."

✦ ✦ ✦

Krause's relationship with Elise Linden and her family had grown stronger despite their distance. Krause became a big brother figure to Joe Linden, who often assisted on his milk delivery routes. Taking advantage of the help, Krause often sent Joe running down alleys and up flights of stairs to deliver the bottles and collect the empties. As a reward, Krause would buy lunch and nickel beers, organizing their route so it ended at the rural summer camp in Palos Hills, where they could swim.

During his summer employment, Krause also became acquainted with an up-and-coming young athlete named George Connor, who became known as "Moose" at DeLaSalle for his dominating line play.

Idolizing Krause while growing up, Connor felt honored to have his hero's nickname bestowed on him. When Krause ambled up to St. Columbanus Parish where Connor worked one summer afternoon, the young lineman seized the opportunity. Krause wanted to speak to the Monsignor about sprinklers. Connor wanted to talk about playing tackle. "We sat and visited for hours," Connor says. "We talked about football, basketball, school and everything. He was something to behold."

Joe Linden likewise had known of Krause through newspaper accounts of his high school and college athletic exploits. Moose's disarming demeanor made him an even bigger man in Joe's eyes. "He was the kindest, nicest, most easygoing person in the world," Linden says. "He got me my first pair of aluminum ice skates . . . and I don't think I'll ever forget, he had a wool camelhair shirt I kept admiring and one day he just took it off and gave it to me."

When Elise and Ed became engaged, news of the impending nuptials made not only the society pages, but even *Chicago Tribune* sports editor Arch Ward's "In the Wake of the News" column. One paper noted, below a photo of the happy couple, "Moose Krause . . . was thrown for a loss (or was it a gain?) by Dan Cupid."

They were married August 27, 1938, at Little Flower Catholic Church, the Linden's neighborhood parish. Elise tossed her bouquet off the back balcony into the backyard of her parents' home, where they held their modest reception in the basement. For their honeymoon, the newlyweds could afford only a long weekend at the Edgewater Beach Hotel in Chicago before setting off for Winona to begin their life together.

Their first year together in Winona would be Krause's best—and last—at Saint Mary's. Though the football team never amounted to much, he coaxed a conference championship out of the basketball team, finishing 10-2 to tie Hamline College for the Minnesota State title. After Frank Vaickus sank a free throw to defeat St. Francis, 41-40, on March 4, 1939, Krause challenged Hamline to a one-game playoff to decide the outright champion. Nobody seemed to know whether he proposed the contest in jest or not, but Hamline coach Joe Hutton apparently took it seriously. He resisted the idea emphatically. "In the first place," Hutton said in the *Winona Republican-Herald,* "we've already beaten St. Mary's this year and I don't see why we have to do it again. Risking the title in such a game would leave us with everything to lose and nothing to gain." With Krause's impending departure to coach at Holy Cross College already public knowledge, he stirred sentiment for a rematch, offering to fly back from Worcester, Massachusetts, anytime the game could be arranged. It never happened, but Saint Mary's athletic growth not only allowed Krause to make the career move to Holy Cross, but left a lasting legacy at Terrace Heights.

"I want particularly to pay a tribute to Coach Ed Krause before he leaves permanently to go to new fields in the East," Saint Mary's president, Brother Leopold, said at the year-end sports banquet. "His record as a gentleman in high school and college is also the record he had among people in Winona, newspaper reporters throughout the state and with all people with whom he has come in contact.

"Mr. Krause is an admirable coach and it is just that he should go higher. . . . About the greatest tribute I can pay to Coach Krause is that he has been a great inspiration in his unpretentious way, and I want to repeat Coach Dave McMillan's words about him . . . 'Notre Dame teams always are courteous and sportsmanlike and the greatest gentlemen of them all was Ed Krause.'"

✦ ✦ ✦

After an icy drive east to snowy Worcester, Mass., in March 1939—Krause's new colleagues joked that he must have brought the weather with him from Minnesota—Ed and Elise settled into their new life in the northeast. Ed liked the looks of the Holy Cross football team he encountered during spring practice. His new boss, Joe Sheeketski, another in a growing legion of Notre Dame–educated professors of football, had assembled a team that, unlike Saint Mary's, at least looked the part. "My, but they're big boys," Ed blurted upon first sight of his strapping tackles. Spring practice, its inherent optimism compounded by the arrival of a new coaching staff, felt like a football rebirth to Krause.

Though they considered living in Chicago for all but the four months of football season, Ed and Elise instead chose to rent a home in Worcester and spend all their time there. They needed the stability because Elise soon became pregnant with their first child. Edward Jr., was born in 1940, filling Krause with visions of another athlete in the family.

Living full time in Worcester also made sense because a revival of the defunct Holy Cross basketball program appeared imminent and Krause figured to be a natural choice as head coach. He also would have ample semi-pro basketball opportunities throughout the northeast, where the once-popular winter pastime needed a boost. Teams, usually sponsored by local businesses or individuals, needed box-office appeal and Krause's basketball reputation preceded him. "Local promoters got wind of Ed's prowess in the hoop game," sports reporter Gerry Moore wrote, "and trampled all over each other trying to secure his services."

On the football field, Holy Cross boasted one of its best lines in years, a strong and agile group that placed an emphasis on precision over power, as so many of Rockne's teams had. With fellow Notre Dame graduate Frank Leahy as head coach at Boston College and Sheeketski and Krause at Holy Cross, college football in the northeast took on a decidedly Irish flavor. As the 1939 season unfolded, excitement for the season finale between Holy Cross and Boston College at Fenway Park built with each passing week. Holy Cross had dominated the series in recent years, and most expected a similar outcome in 1939, though the success of both teams foreshadowed an exciting battle.

Joe Nolan, writing in the Holy Cross student publication *The Tomahawk,* fed the hype with direct comparisons to the Irish. "It's a tribute to Joe Sheeketski and to his team to say that they play Notre Dame football in the Notre Dame way. . . . No greater praise could be heaped upon any team." After a 46-0 thrashing of Providence a week before the showdown with Boston College, Nolan echoed the purple prose of Grantland Rice, writing "Today they stand out from the cleated herd in bold relief, silhouetted against the November sky—Holy Cross, the best in the East."

Foreshadowing the "fanatical determination" that would ultimately drive him from football, Leahy vomited the morning before his first game as Boston College head coach, against a team called Lebanon Valley State. Imagine how his insides must have churned the week before the game against heavily favored rival Holy Cross. Leahy had been so paranoid about the game he sent his nephew to spy on the Crusaders practices, according to Twombley in *Shake Down the Thunder.* He appeared distant and distracted at a meeting with football writers the Monday before the game. Sheeketski's comparatively cool demeanor suggested a Holy Cross swagger that would carry over to the field on Saturday, continuing the Crusaders' recent domination of this passionate series.

A persistent, spitting snow muddied the field at Fenway Park, neutralizing Holy Cross' star halfback Ronnie Cahill. It did not disrupt Boston College. In another glimpse of Leahy's coaching future, he treated his football hypochondria with obsessive preparation, producing surgical precision on the field in a 14-0 win over Holy Cross, only the second loss of the season for the Crusaders. On the way to the locker room afterward, Twombly reports, a frustrated Sheeketski turned to an assistant coach and said, "That God damned Leahy out-coached me. Don't ask me how he did it. He just did."

✦ ✦ ✦

In the midst of all the football excitement, Holy Cross announced plans to reinstate its basketball program with Krause as the coach. A decade earlier, administrators decided to eliminate the sport because of a lack of a suitable on-campus facility. Though they had little more than an optimistic proposal for a new fieldhouse in 1939, they decided to begin the rebuilding process, hoping success would coincide with the opening of a new building two or three years hence.

That fledgling team would not begin playing until February, with a modest schedule to ease its way back to a competitive level. That gave Krause ample time to explore semi-pro basketball opportunities among several regional teams anxious for his services.

He played for as many as four teams at once, drawing $50–$100 per game for his commanding combination of size, strength and deftness with the ball. In an era when offenses weaved around a center making deceptive pivot moves before passing to a darting teammate or taking a shot, Krause defined the position. His size made him a huge target under the basket. His strength allowed him to overpower opponents for rebounds. His agility fooled defenders and created dazzling shots and passes that sold tickets from Boston Garden to Pawtucket to Portland, Maine. "As unpredictable as April weather," went one account, "he either passed sharply to one of his mates or suddenly pivoted and shot for the hoop, but his foes never could guess which he planned to do."

His performances proved worth the price of admission in towns around the region. He scored 27 points for the Boston Good-Wins in a victory at Haverhill and repeated that feat in wins at Pawtucket and Rockland, where fans had to be turned away.

A team called the Hull Collegians, from New Haven, ventured into Worcester's Mechanics Hall to play the Good-Wins one winter afternoon with an imposing resume of twenty-two wins without a loss. "A positive 'must' for every dyed-in-the-wool court follower," one newspaper promised, this game would truly measure Krause's talent. In its next edition, the paper proclaimed, "Any remaining doubt that Ed 'Moose' Krause is the greatest individual court star Boston has seen in many years was dispelled yesterday afternoon at Mechanics Building when he chalked up 30 points to lead the Good-Wins to a soft 73-40 victory over the Hull Collegians of New Haven."

Later in the season, the Good-Wins visited New Haven and Krause scored 28 more in another hard lesson for the Hull Collegians. The Good-Wins then traveled overnight to Portland, Maine, where a weary Krause played only the second half the next evening, "entering the game when his team was trailing and sparking it to a win."

Krause's agreement to play for two Worcester teams excited the local papers and inspired apathetic fans. When the newly organized Worcester Pros prepared to open play at Mechanics Hall, everyone knew that "Ed Krause . . . will be the big magnet at the Main-Street edifice." Fans crowded outside Mechanics Hall to see his inaugural game with the Pros, though logistical and promotional problems kept the doors closed until fifteen minutes after the scheduled tip-off and drove many away. Six hundred fans stayed to see Krause score 12 of his team's 35 points, including the game-winning basket, in a two-point victory over the Harlem Yankees.

In addition to his schedule with the Good-Wins and the Pros, Krause also signed with the persistent and generous Narcus Bros. Stationers, another Worcester-based team. He yielded to repeated overtures from sponsor Jake Narcus, agreeing in mid-December to join the team after the Christmas holiday for $100 per game. Krause would later say he named a price far beyond what he imagined Narcus would pay just to fend off his advances. Much to Krause's surprise, and delight, Narcus agreed to his terms.

"Beaming all over," Narcus announced the acquisition of Krause, a move that would alter the balance of power in the competitive Worcester city league. Norton Co. had dominated for years, on the strength of its own star center, Mutt Johnson. Narcus Bros. fielded competitive teams but failed to derail Norton's perennial superiority. To Jake Narcus, $100 a game seemed a small price to pay to end that frustration.

By day, Krause cobbled together and polished the pieces to restore the Holy Cross basketball program. By night, he toured the northeast, a freelance center of sorts, offering his considerable services to teams in need of victories and paying customers. Krause delivered both.

When basketball practice ended for the Crusaders in the late afternoon, Krause caught a commuter train or a ride from a teammate or a family member to wherever he had a game that night. Elise often drove him, allowing Ed to curl his oversized frame into the backseat for a quick nap, while infant Eddie cradled up front next to his mother. Sometimes Elise's younger brother, Joe Linden, who lived with the Krauses in Worcester while he attended Holy Cross, did the driving for him around wintry New England.

Once on the court, Krause earned the money promoters like Jake Narcus clamored to pay him. His success with the Narcus Bros. over the final two months of the 1940 season stirred a raging debate around Worcester. Moose Krause or Mutt Johnson? Newcomer or established star? Who would win the anticipated showdown between the Moose and the Mutt? Everybody had an opinion and shared it in bars and barber shops around town until February 27 when "these semi-pro titans" collided in Worcester's South High gym. Somehow 1,900 fans squeezed into a room designed for several hundred fewer. Sports reporter Louis Kursman captured the spirit of the moment in the next day's newspaper:

In a blazingly brilliant basketball battle waged before a roaring overflow crowd which threatened to burst South High gymnasium at the seams, Narcus Bros. defeated Nortons last night and vaulted ahead in the high-tension race for the city semi-pro championship.

The score was 44 to 40.

Nineteen hundred fans, jammed in the seats, packed in the aisles and hanging on the girders, saw . . . those two strapping gentlemen of definite stamina, Ed Krause, the Moose, and Howard Johnson, the Mutt, locked in their widely-heralded center duel. And Narcus fans gilded Krause's name with acclaim as he outplayed the crack Norton pivot man who experienced his worst shooting night in years . . .

Krause clamped his 225 pounds on Johnson like a leech from start to last. The big Norton center went without a goal from the floor and his total for the night was a free throw which came midway in the first period in which he missed seven pegs.

Krause, high gun in almost every game he has competed this season, again made off with individual scoring laurels. He pumped in five field goals and three penalty shots for 13 points.

An editorial cartoon under the headline, "THE TOWN'S STILL TALKING," depicted a towering Krause reaching eagerly over a stunned Norton player, his huge hands about to seize a glittering symbol of the city title. But the Narcus Bros. team would have to win a playoff rematch against Norton three weeks later to secure that championship. Krause reprised his earlier performance, outscoring Johnson 13-5 in a 47-38 win, firmly establishing himself as the region's best player and inspiring even more applause from the local papers:

Back in January Narcus Bros. hitched their basketball wagon to a star named Ed Krause and dividends were paid off last night in the shape of the city semi-pro championship. Mighty precious dividends too, it might be added, since the losers were nobody else but the Norton Grinders, who have been kingpins of the roost for more seasons than a fellow can remember offhand. Krause came to town heralded as one of the finest hunks of hoop flesh ever to pop out of the Middle West and he was all of that in last night's title duel. . . . In the final analysis of the Narcus Bros. first championship, one always must come back to Krause. He made victory possible.

Krause's mere presence did not have such a profound effect on the Holy Cross basketball teams he coached. Much like his football teams at Saint Mary's, the Crusaders suffered from slim pickings on the court. They had talent but not depth, a deficiency exacerbated by a lack of on-campus facilities that made practices inconvenient and the future of the program questionable. "Instead of inviting boys out for the team," Joe Nolan wrote in the Holy Cross student paper, "[Krause] has to dare them to report."

Plans for a new fieldhouse did not proceed with the expected speed. With the one court on campus in a temporary gym dedicated to intramural sports, Krause had to take his team to a high school in town for workouts and on the road for games. "This set-up," Nolan continued in his criticism of administrative reticence to provide the program with the necessary infrastructure, "is about as popular with the players as a corsage of poison ivy would be with your best girl. . . . A day of reckoning must come soon when the [athletic administrators] will have to decide whether they want to have two Intramural leagues, with one of them masquerading under the name of a varsity basketball squad, or whether they are going to permit the Krausemen to take precedence over all other court activities."

Basketball never took precedence or gained prominence with Krause at the helm, but he built quite a foundation for the future. Against mediocre competition, Holy Cross had only modest success in Krause's three seasons, winning less than half its games. Within five years, though, the Crusaders would be national champions, securing basketball's status on campus.

Meanwhile, the football team foundered. After Sheeketski's initial 7-2 season in 1939 ended with the demoralizing loss to Boston College, his team staggered to just eight wins over the next two years combined. Krause gave the Crusaders some hope for the future with his persistent recruitment of George Connor, who had blossomed into a star worthy of the "Moose" nickname. They had developed a friendly relationship through the years during Krause's visits to Chicago. "I don't think many prep athletes had the attention that I had from a recruiter," Connor says.

"I'll be with you night and day at Holy Cross," Krause said.

Already interested in Holy Cross because of a long-standing family connection, Connor needed no more prodding. He committed to becoming a Crusader.

Swirling rumors intensified around Mt. St. James that Sheeketski would be sacked when the 1941 season ended, putting his assistants' future in doubt as well. Speculation soon turned into reality, leaving Krause to wonder what the next football season would bring for him.

Frank Leahy's fast-rising star had taken him to Notre Dame in 1941 and, as luck would have it, he needed a line coach the following year. Leahy invited Krause to his hotel suite at a coaches' convention that winter. Leahy summoned Krause to Notre Dame with an offer to be an assistant football and basketball coach. A tearful Krause immediately accepted and called his wife. "Mother," he choked through the phone line, using the term of endearment he had bestowed on her since the birth of Eddie, "we're going home."

✦ ✦ ✦

So much for Krause's promise to Connor. "I was on the New York Central going out to Holy Cross," Connor says, "while Moose Krause and Elise and family were on the train going west."

Returning to Notre Dame as a coach fulfilled Krause's career aspirations before he turned thirty. Married to the only woman he ever loved, with a young son he envisioned as a future Irish athletic star, and a job he coveted since the day he graduated, Krause felt truly rooted for the first time.

Elise ruled their new Chester Street roost on the east side of South Bend, organizing their home and family activities in her firm and efficient fashion. That left Krause free, for want of a better term, to become indentured to Leahy for several months a year. After hours of cracking heads with strapping tackles on the practice field, evaluating their development down to the most minuscule detail and watching more film than a Hollywood director, Leahy finally released his assistants.

Leahy worked himself even harder, instituting a T-formation offense much to fans' consternation at the start of the 1942 season. The famous, and familiar, Rockne shift had worked for years, so why tamper with it, they wondered aloud. After the team opened with a tie at Wisconsin and a loss at home against Georgia Tech, the criticism became incessant and the stress overcame the coach. A spinal arthritis condition forced him to spend three weeks at the Mayo Clinic.

Assistant coach Ed McKeever steered the Irish to three victories, with Leahy in frequent contact by telephone during the week to tweak the game plan. As Jack Connor writes in *Leahy's Lads*, the time away allowed him to ponder the team's problems from an objective distance and introduce a seemingly minor wrinkle in the play-calling system that had major implications. Notre Dame won seven of its last nine games, propelling Leahy and the Irish toward one of the most prosperous periods in college football history.

After home football games, Notre Dame coaches and their families, along with university officials and representatives of the visiting team, often gathered at the Krauses' home for cocktails. Even Leahy had an occasional drink, though he usually corralled his assistants in the attic to discuss strategy for the next week after making a polite appearance among the guests.

As she had since they were married, Elise handled the household chores, paid the bills and made most of the decisions that affected the family. Krause, meanwhile, spent as much time away from home as he did during his barnstorming basketball days back in Worcester. Recruiting, scouting, traveling with the football and basketball teams and long hours in the office kept him as busy as he had ever been, though he ostensibly had fewer responsibilities than he did at Saint Mary's and Holy Cross. Leahy demanded Krause's undivided attention from September through December, and again during spring practice, while basketball coach George Keogan filled the months in between with his own fidgeting and fussing.

A twenty-year veteran on the Irish sidelines, Keogan had not mellowed over time. Heart problems compelled doctors to restrict his activities, but once a basketball game began, he could not be restrained. "As a bench flutter-budget Keogan has few equals," newspaper reporter Lyall Smith wrote. A photo accompanying Smith's article shows Keogan coiled on the bench, his right hand clenched, his eyes anxiously scanning the action, as if he might spring out of his seat at any moment. Krause sits alongside his boss, a concerned look on his face, but with his chin in his hand like "The Thinker," looking as relaxed as Keogan appears restless.

Keogan had little reason to worry. His 1942–43 team won twelve of its first thirteen games with a handful of potent scorers, including a 74-43 win over an undefeated New York University team at Madison Square Garden. "He was a proud man," says Bob Rensberger, one of the leading scorers on that team, "and he was so happy with that victory."

An animated Keogan conducted practice as usual after the team returned from New York, even demonstrating drills, a rarity since health problems slowed him years earlier. "He should not have been coaching," Rensberger says. "He was told by the doctors that he should not coach and if he continued to coach, he could very easily have a problem. I guess he thought if he gave up coaching, why, he couldn't do that."

Instead, Keogan coached until the day he died. After returning home from practice on February 17, 1943, he ate dinner and settled into a comfortable chair to read the newspaper. Keogan's wife, Ruby, heard their dog whining and walked from the kitchen to find her husband slumped over in his chair, dead of a massive heart attack at age fifty-two.

With his players as pallbearers, Keogan was buried on a Saturday morning and the emotional Irish then traveled to Chicago for a game that night against Great Lakes. As a tribute to Notre Dame's fallen coach, the lights at Chicago Stadium were dimmed and a spotlight shone on an empty chair on their bench, where Keogan would have been.

Krause stepped in as interim head coach. Notre Dame, the sentimental favorite of the 15,000 who filled Chicago Stadium, may have felt the hand of fate after Frannie Curran's shot at the buzzer sent the game into overtime. Their emotional energy spent, the Irish could not maintain the pace and lost in the extra session. Regrouping to win its final five games to finish at 18-2, Keogan's final team left a legacy as one of the best in the nation. Notre Dame's long-standing prohibition on postseason play, an attempt to keep athletics in proper perspective, denied the team the opportunity to validate its reputation.

In an announcement expected for months, Krause was named the permanent replacement for Keogan in May. As part of the promotion, he also became an instructor for the university's wartime training program, an increasingly prominent presence on campus.

World War II changed Notre Dame forever. Struggling financially at the time, the university became indebted to the United States Navy, which opened a training base at Notre Dame, sending an infusion of sailors and tax dollars. That forged an enduring relationship between the two institutions, preserved in the annual football series between the Irish and the Midshipmen.

Of course, the war disrupted the lives of virtually every young man enrolled at Notre Dame. Even star quarterback and Heisman Trophy winner Angelo Bertelli was called into active service in the Marine Corps before the end of the 1943 national championship season. As the war effort intensified and more players went overseas, it became clear to Krause that he and Leahy would have to enlist, for reasons as pragmatic as they were patriotic. Leahy resisted at first, but Krause convinced him that players returning from the war would not respect them if they had not done their part. How could they be leaders to men who had postponed their futures and risked their lives, Krause insisted, if they had not? Within a year, both men would be aboard ships bound for the South Pacific.

CHAPTER

4

A Joy Boy of Emirau

HUNDREDS OF NORMALLY ROWDY YOUNG MARINES stood silently at the rail of the troop transport Sea Cat departing November 1, 1944, from Miramar Naval Base near San Diego. They watched the southern California coastline—and by extension, their friends, families and life as they knew it—disappear behind them. A secret South Pacific location and an unknown fate lay ahead.

Second lieutenant Krause sensed the apprehension in the silence. He felt it himself. In all his years of barnstorming basketball and relentless recruiting trips, he had left Elise and Eddie for maybe a weekend at a time, a week at most. This journey would separate them indefinitely, perhaps forever. That agonizing reality sunk in as the ship pushed out to sea, to war, toward an island and an experience more exotic, more mysterious, more dangerous than anything he ever imagined.

Several months of training at Quonset Point, Rhode Island, taught Krause the principles of combat intelligence. It could not instill the courage necessary to endure the mental strain of applying those principles in life-and-death situations. With his friend and Notre Dame classmate Johnny McLaughlin hosting Elise and Eddie at his Rhode Island home not far from Quonset Point, Krause had the companionship of his family to comfort him during training. Nothing could prepare him for the emotional pangs he felt with the incomprehensible vastness of the Pacific Ocean between them.

Riding west from Rhode Island to Miramar aboard a Rock Island Line train in September, Krause wrestled with the innocent question a disappointed Eddie, about to turn four years old, asked before he left.

"Why won't you be at my birthday party?"

He answered with a heartfelt letter, explaining his absence to Eddie, justifying it to himself.

September 9, 1944

I want so much to be with you and Mother at the party, but I have some important work to do, so I had to leave, which was one of the hardest things I've ever had to do in my life. . . . Sometimes in life, son, you may have to do things you won't want to. If such a time ever comes, remember this—No matter how hard a problem confronts you, if you do it for someone you love it is worth your every effort.

God only knows where I will go or what I will do. But wherever I go and whatever I do, I will be happy because I will be doing it for your Mother and you, my son. You are my life and all I live for . . .

Your Lonely Dad

Once he set out for the South Pacific, Krause occupied himself with multiple tasks aboard the Sea Cat, submerging his loneliness in duty. He broadcast a morning news report in addition to serving as the welfare, morale and assistant chaplain officer, organizing calisthenics, entertainment and religious services during the three-week passage. At night, in a cramped berth not built to accommodate a man of his bulk, Krause compiled a hybrid of a journal and a letter home, in a script alternately smooth and ragged depending on the mood of the sea.

Nov. 1, 1944

When I looked back at San Diego on the horizon, I said, "Kid, we're not playing anymore, this is the real thing" . . . as we left the shore of our homes, there was no shouting or singing. It was quiet on the ship, the older me looked back stoically to shore, the younger men . . . stopped chatting and looked back. Silence prevailed—some left wives and children behind, others mothers and sweethearts—we all left some-one behind. Yep! We have a lot to fight for—a lot to come back to. . . . I'll try to be the busiest man on this ship to keep from loneliness and selfishness. . . . I really am glad we left today. This is All-Saints Day, so we have all the saints with us.

Reveille rousted the Marines at 6:30 the next morning, a calm, sunny day at sea. Many men felt seasick from their first night on board, despite relatively smooth sailing. Krause felt "grand." After breakfast at 7:30, he worked in the chaplain's office until noon, with a few minutes off to deliver the day's news. In the afternoon, he auditioned Marines with musical talent to perform on what would become a promenade deck of sorts aboard a heavily armed cruise ship. He also recruited any-one with technical aptitude to run the movie projectors. And he led all three calisthenics sessions himself. Distractions. Anything to keep his mind from wandering home.

Krause felt an aching loneliness at night, struggling to sleep in his confining berth, with only a pen, paper and photos of Elise and Eddie for companionship. His correspondence, which could not be sent home at least until a day ashore in Hawaii later in the month, served as therapy for Krause as much as communication with his wife and son. He confided and complained in those pages, venting anger that he enlisted and left home at an age when many of his peers avoided service. He felt abandoned by friends in the months after he left home for training, hurt and angry that many who endured no disruption to their lives did not take the time to wish him well. A rare occasion of frustration and self-pity came over Krause just before he boarded the Sea Cat, and it spilled onto the pages of his journal. "Why should I be going away when I know of many guys back home who just figure this is another man's war, not theirs?" he lamented to himself as he prepared to ship out. "I don't feel bad about going, but it sure burns you up."

Mostly, Krause used his journal to console himself with a connection, however slight, to his wife and son, "who miss me if I'm gone a weekend." His words often took on a certain intimacy, as if he was whispering to Elise instead of writing to her.

Nov. 2, 1944

I miss you dear, and spend many hours during the day and evening just thinking of you and Eddie, wondering what you are doing—wishing I was with you. All I hope for is to come back soon. Good night, dear. I love you and miss you.

With ocean waves rising on their third day out and the ship rolling violently as a storm approached, everyone's attention turned to a suspected enemy submarine ahead. After frenzied precautionary procedures and time-consuming evasive maneuvers, after everything had been secured and everyone had been ordered below decks, they discovered it had been a false alarm and returned to their routine duties. But the threat of just such an encounter remained very real, adding time and tension to an already long and emotionally draining journey. They traveled a deliberately random zig-zag path in the general direction of their

destination to avoid the Japanese "submarine menace," a necessary tactic that made their passage maddeningly slow. All the well-trained
Marines had to fight off boredom, more than enemy bombardment, as
they crossed the Pacific.

A group of Marines listened to the Georgia-Alabama football
broadcast over short wave radio the next morning. The Notre Dame-
Navy game could not be picked up, except for the score, 32-13 in favor
of the Midshipmen over the service-depleted Irish. "That was too bad
but if you remember I expected this," Krause wrote. "Now I'm afraid
of the Army, Great Lakes and Georgia Tech. We should lose three of
those four." He sat down to write early that Saturday because the movie
that evening, *Casablanca,* would not end until after lights out and he
wanted to see Bogey and Bacall again. He also had to prepare prayer services for the following morning.

Krause's vision of himself as a priest had faded in the decade since
his father's death, but his devotion to the Church never diminished. He
considered Mass and Communion as integral to his spiritual well-being
as three meals a day to his physical health. Krause relished this opportunity to stand before his fellow Marines at a time when many might feel
their faith waver, reassuring them with familiar rituals and the comforting feel of a Rosary between their fingers. He chose prayers and readings for his "Mass" carefully, presenting them with an earnest reverence
he reserved for matters of faith. Two candles and a crucifix served as
the altar—"beautiful in its simplicity," he noted in his journal—around
which hundreds of men gathered on their first Sunday morning at sea
for services Krause led in lieu of an ordained priest.

Nov. 5, 1944

It really was an inspiration to me. . . . It was the greatest
honor and pleasure I have ever had. I selected the Rosary,
Epistle, Gospel and the Litany of the Blessed Virgin as the

best possible service we could hold, besides we also said an Act of Contrition. I just can't forget the faces of the boys as they followed me in prayer. They were hungry for Mass and Communion. . . . As far as I was concerned, I don't know when I was closer to God.

Yet Krause had never felt so far from home. His tour of duty had hardly begun. Four days at sea and they had not even set foot on the Hawaiian islands, where the Sea Cat would rendezvous with its escort to the South Pacific. "How I yearn for my family," he wrote. "This is the longest I have ever been away from them in all my life and to think it's going to be twenty times longer or more. I know I'll come home, when? God only knows. Please God, no matter what I do, help me be a credit to God, my country and my loved ones."

Krause did not include the Notre Dame football team in his prayers. Even divine intervention hardly could have helped that cause, though the Irish succeeded far beyond Krause's minimal expectations during the war-ravaged 1944 season. Ed McKeever coached the team in Leahy's absence. He accepted the thankless role of keeping Leahy's seat warm during the war, with every able-bodied young man either overseas or enrolled at a military academy. He never had a chance to match "The Master's" success. McKeever knew it. Krause knew it. Even the rabid Notre Dame football fans knew it. With a war on, the mortal sin of losing a football game became merely venial.

Not that Notre Dame lost many under McKeever, an assistant to Leahy since his days at Boston College. McKeever had to replace several stars from the 1943 national championship team now in the service with a group of freshmen and military rejects. Yet after a 64-0 thrashing of Dartmouth lifted Notre Dame's record to 3-0, newspapers started calling McKeever "another Leahy." He won two more, over Wisconsin and Illinois, before the honeymoon ended, as expected, against Navy's arsenal. Army awaited the following week, playing in honor of former Cadet star and assistant coach Colonel Red Reeder, who lost his left leg in the Normandy invasion and watched from a wheelchair at midfield.

Krause cringed as he listened to the Cadets, at the height of their football power, overwhelm his beloved Irish. He heard Doc Blanchard and Glenn Davis punish Notre Dame with run after demoralizing run, inflicting the worst defeat in Irish history, 59-0. "I was very disappointed," Krause wrote. "I knew we'd lose but not by that large a score."

He considered the war an extended recruiting trip of sorts, always keeping an eye open for potential football talent and trying to win more fans over to Notre Dame's burgeoning national base. He absorbed considerable ribbing for the monumental margin of defeat against Army, but Krause seldom dwelled on the details of wins and losses, a trait that hindered him as a coach. He preferred to focus on the bigger picture of competition and camaraderie, a trait that drew so many people to him, and by extension to Notre Dame. Mainly, though, Krause just enjoyed convivial company over cocktails.

A handful of Marines learned that firsthand during a day of liberty on Pearl Harbor. They had not seen land for a week and did not waste a moment of their time ashore. Disembarking in the morning, with twelve hours to themselves, they sought good food and copious drink wherever it could be found. "We had steak for lunch & dinner, 10 beers and a few high balls," Krause wrote, with a few uncharacteristically crossed-out words—slurred script—offering evidence of their exploits. "It was swell setting foot on land." Those feet stumbled unsteadily back to the ship that night to resume their journey to the South Pacific.

✦ ✦ ✦

Back aboard the Sea Cat, Krause remained a mere Pollywog, Marine-speak for a man who has not yet crossed the Equator, a rite of passage rife with initiation rituals. At age 31, he did not relish the idea of being the butt of any military-style fraternity pranks. A man of his size, of course, seldom has to endure such indignities. Krause devised a counteroffensive with Bill Osmanski, a military dentist and former All-American fullback at Holy Cross, to avoid spending a single night in the brig to be anointed a Shellback. It had none of the nuance of a Leahy-designed game plan—just sheer force and the element of surprise—but it worked equally well.

The Sea Cat crossed the Equator at 2:30 P.M. on November 13. "There was to have been an initiation," Krause wrote, "but Bill Osmanski and I ruined their plans by putting all [Shellback] men in the brig." His casual reference to their surprise attack belies the intense, if light-hearted, nature of the battle. Peter Ingberg, a Marine pilot from Minnesota, remembers about thirty-five officers, all Pollywogs including Krause and Osmanski, descending upon the outnumbered Shellbacks. They grabbed two men each, wrestling them down a ladder to the brig. Resistant victims to this breach of tradition, some Shellbacks "grabbed each officers' legs—which didn't faze the two All-Americans," Ingberg says. "Down the ladder the two went, [taking] the Shellbacks to the brig and [locking] them up." They returned to the top deck several times to repeat this process until the captain of the ship ordered the fighting to stop and declared all Pollywogs official Shellbacks. "So now I have graduated," Krause noted proudly in his journal, "from a poor Pollywog to a genuine Shellback."

Krause's willingness to tweak military tradition and his talent for creating diversions to occupy anxious or idle Marines would become a welcome antidote to the occasionally tense, often tedious, reality of war.

✦ ✦ ✦

Assigned to Marine Bomber Squadron 413, Krause served on Emirau in the Solomon Islands. It served as a base of continuous air assaults

against Rabaul, described in *Leatherneck* magazine as "the bustling, burgeoning center of Japanese military power" in the South Pacific. More
than 180,000 Japanese soldiers and 300 enemy aircraft operated from
the former British colonial center on the eastern end of New Britain
Island. Rabaul's two harbors allowed Japan to control the region from
the moment it seized the city in 1942.

An Allied invasion to recapture Rabaul appeared inevitable. Imperial
forces on the imposing, powerfully fortified base braced for an attack,
preparing to defend their island to the last man. Edwin P. Hoyt, in *The
Glory of the Solomons*, called this stubborn resistance to an invasion that
would never come, "General Imamura's miscalculation." Vanquished
General Tojo later told the victorious General MacArthur that "the one
great unexpected move the Allies had made was to bypass the strongest
Japanese base system in the Pacific."

After a costly invasion of the nearby island of Bougainville, Allied
strategists determined a D-Day style storming of Rabaul's beaches
would be unnecessarily perilous. They decided instead "to destroy
Rabaul's offensive capability and seal off the base from reinforcement."
Marines on Emirau played a central role in this strategy to render the
Rabaul arsenal impotent through relentless bombing, allowing the Allies
to advance toward Tokyo.

Emirau fell to the Allies in March 1944, completing the noose tight-
ening around the Japanese stronghold. Air strikes against Rabaul, under-
way for months from other islands, began almost immediately from the
makeshift runways of Emirau. By the time Krause arrived in November,
Rabaul already had been effectively neutralized. He and his unit would
be charged with maintaining its isolation. "Allied leaders and men who
took part in the campaign against Rabaul passed on to more active
fronts," notes the *History of Marine Corps Operations in World War II*.
"Those who remained had the thankless task of keeping the Japanese
beaten down."

One by one, all day and all night, B-25s revved their engines, rumbled down the runway and roared off toward Rabaul with a payload designed to destroy morale as much as ammunition. It took that kind of relentless action to make Japanese will so much as waver. Though their offensive potential lay in ruins, formidable anti-aircraft weapons remained on Rabaul, "a strong steel umbrella over the target," and the remaining Imperial soldiers still stood ready for battle. They relished nothing more than knocking one of the Allied planes always buzzing overhead into the Pacific.

Krause's assignment as a combat intelligence officer was to plan the air raids and send Marines on the safest, most efficient missions possible. He culled information for his daily briefings from a variety of sources—from traditional military intelligence and maps of the region, from conversations and excursions with pilots, and from the native Moro people he befriended. A frail, diminutive population, the Moro were in awe of Krause, especially a young man named Antoun, who would play an integral role in the American war effort on Emirau. "He looked up to Big Ed as someone from *outer space*," says the company chaplain, Rev. James Gannon, who learned the impact of Krause's size firsthand immediately after their introduction.

Gannon had been on Emirau several months before Krause arrived. He offered daily services in a chapel made of coconut logs with a coral floor covered in sand so the men would not cut their knees when they knelt in prayer. The Naval Construction Battalion, known as the Seabees, who maintained roads and runways and fresh-water systems, helped Gannon construct the chapel with materials from their supply ship. As a finishing flourish, they added an altar railing carved from tree branches. "It was beautifully done," Gannon says.

The chapel was one of the first places Krause visited when he arrived on Emirau. He offered to serve Mass for Gannon, but the chaplain said he already had enough help, so Krause took his place among the congregation. "At Communion time, as he knelt down on the step and leaned on the altar railing, the whole thing collapsed," Gannon says. "There was a loud noise and I turned around and there he was, big as he was, face down in the sand. Everybody started to laugh and he was completely covered over with the branches used for the altar railing. I told Moose from that time on he would serve my Mass, but that he would have to kneel up straight and not lean on anything."

Despite this unsteady start, Krause became an officer other Marines leaned on. His briefings, given alongside the runway in a small "Intelligence Hut" constructed in the same makeshift manner as the chapel, offered motivation as much as information. They were the pep talks he never found the words to deliver in a locker room. With so much more at stake than wins and losses, Krause offered tactical details with Leahy's precision, encouraged pilots with Rockne's flair, and lightened the mood as only Moose himself could. "He always had a great sense of humor," says Tom Clemente, a navigator-bombardier and budding baseball player from New York, who Krause recruited to Notre Dame. "If he could give it a light touch, that would always be there. The other guys would be pretty somber."

No matter how many missions they flew, the pilots always felt anxious about the next one. Some fidgeted as their flights approached, others smoked or talked nervously, trying to think about anything but the terrible, unspoken possibility hanging as heavily in the air as airplane exhaust. Once they lifted off the island, they might never return. Krause's variety-show briefings became a welcome distraction.

One evening before a particularly important and dangerous raid under cover of darkness, the tension in the Intelligence Hut was palpable. "You could see they weren't themselves," Gannon says. "Moose had anticipated this happening." So he planned a surprise as both an inspiration and a calming influence. Krause brought in about twenty Moro natives—scouts for the Americans who gathered intelligence information and searched for downed pilots in the disorienting terrain. Each of the Marines at the briefing expected the same routine they had heard several times before. "If you get lost or in trouble," Krause had reminded them over and over, "they'll find you and bring you back safely." This time, though, he turned to the young Moro men, and with a gesture of his hand and a, "One, two, three," they broke into the Notre Dame Victory March in their native language. "The whole group of two hundred men went berserk," Gannon says. "The laughing and cheering and whistling—they couldn't believe it."

Colonel P.K. Smith, commanding officer of the squadron, could not believe it either. He considered the impending mission among the most important of their campaign and this serenade a frivolous, dangerous distraction. "These fellows are joking and laughing!" the incredulous colonel shouted, unexpectedly entering the hut. "They're in no frame of mind to go out on this raid." Krause felt it was exactly what they needed to relieve the tension. He promised to take the blame if the raid failed. "The next morning when they came back, not a single [man] was lost," Gannon says, praising Krause's intuition. "They were completely at ease—if he had sent them out nervous and tense, quite a few might have been lost."

Krause understood the pressures his pilots faced because he flew with them from time to time. They would climb into their cockpits wearing heavy coveralls and an emergency parachute, armed with a gunbelt and a revolver. Krause squeezed through the narrow passage to the navigator-bombardier station in the nose of the B-25s, an area so small he had to strip down to his shorts just to fit. No parachute, no ammunition, hardly any clothes on his back. "Ed was so large," says Hicks Smith Jr., a pilot from Alabama who Krause occasionally accompanied, "it took him about ten minutes to crawl through."

On those missions, Krause could do his own reconnaissance work. He developed not only an understanding of enemy targets, but also an intimate knowledge of the dangers the pilots dealt with every day—from experience, not from the safe distance of a debriefing. By now, Marines seldom faced enemy fire, as Rabaul and other targets in the region were methodically neutralized. "I flew fifty-eight missions," Clemente says, "and if we had flack twenty times, that was a lot."

After narrowly evading anti-aircraft fire one afternoon on a flight with Smith, however, Krause never flew another mission. His size essentially would have trapped him if an evacuation ever became necessary, a danger too great for an intelligence officer to face on a regular basis. "We finally decided it would be too risky for Ed to be in the nose," Smith says, "so operations grounded him."

Krause grew close to Antoun, a young leader among the Moro people on Emirau. He displayed uncommon courage in assisting the Allies and a deep Catholic faith. Both qualities endeared him to Krause. Educated by Catholic missionaries before the war, Antoun often attended Mass in the Marine chapel, interpreting the Latin service for other Moro natives. In return for this fellowship, Antoun and other Moro people, who could move freely among the natives on Rabaul, offered to serve as scouts for the Marines. Krause often took a group in a PT boat from Emirau to a spot about a mile off the shore of Rabaul. The Moro people would swim ashore to spy on Japanese soldiers and collect information to aid in planning the Marine air raids. A night or two later, Krause would pick them up at the same offshore spot for the ride back to Emirau. Antoun always provided valuable information. He informed Krause of a diversionary Japanese tactic of storing ammunition in hospital tents and housing wounded soldiers and prisoners of war in facilities that appeared from the air to be weapons depots.

After one such mission to Rabaul, Antoun returned with the news of a crude gravesite where the bodies of six Marines had been discarded. He offered to lead Krause and Gannon to their fallen comrades to retrieve their remains for a proper burial. They set out in a PT boat with Antoun guiding them to a safe landing spot on the enemy island. A group of natives then led them along a river in a canoe and up a mountainside to the spot where the bodies lay covered with palm branches.

Darkness fell before they could return, so Krause and Gannon, with the remains of the Marines, followed Antoun to a small village along the coast to spend the night. Antoun assured the apprehensive Americans that they would be safe. "How could that be?" Gannon wondered to himself. "We're on an enemy island." They slept uneasily, but undisturbed, discovering at dawn that they were in a leper colony, an area of the island the Japanese never approached. In gratitude for this safe haven, Krause and Gannon gathered blankets, clothing, medicine and food from the Marines on Emirau to distribute among the ailing men and women whose presence protected them for the night.

They buried the Marines in a cemetery on Emirau with white crosses marking each grave, except for a Jewish comrade, who they laid to rest beneath a Star of David. Gannon not only ministered to the Marines, he served as a missionary of sorts to natives in the region, baptizing babies and performing marriages. Krause often went along as godfather or best man. They even helped foster Antoun's vocation to the priesthood, persuading Bishop Thomas Wade of New Zealand to accept him as a seminarian and organizing a collection among the Marines to pay for his education. "At the end of the day," Gannon says, "we had over two thousand dollars."

These shared spiritual experiences brought Krause and Gannon closer to each other than anyone else on Emirau. That and, as Krause joked for years afterward, "the chaplain had the only cold beer on the island." They stayed up nights drinking, talking football and playing pinochle for islands on a map of the region.

✦ ✦ ✦

As important as his intelligence duties were, Krause perhaps made his most valuable contribution to the war effort in his de facto role as morale officer. He organized the construction of an officers' club on Emirau, a sheet metal structure that resembled a storage depot more than a bar, though it served a far more important function than a warehouse. No lives were saved during the long, lively nights the Marines spent in the officers' club, and no strategic military objectives were achieved, but many spirits were lifted—literally and figuratively.

Whiskey went for five cents a shot in small tin cups, the same for a bottle of beer, necessary to wash down the aftertaste of three daily meals with a Spam main course—and to dull the senses to the sound of the house band, the Joy Boys. Krause, drawing on his brief, unexceptional musical background, strummed a bass fiddle and sang along with the group, which opened each night's performance with the refrain:

We are the Joy Boys of Emirau
We're here to say, 'How do you do?'

The Basie band they were not, but with the booze flowing plentifully, it never seemed to matter. The Joy Boys provided a warbling soundtrack for Marines commiserating over drinks during their free time. Krause and pilot Peter Ingberg, in particular, often held up the bar long into the night. "You might say," Ingberg says, "that Ed and I came to be good barroom buddies." Often after last call, Krause would steady himself with his hand on Ingberg's head as they navigated their way back to their tents, stifling their boozy laughter to avoid disturbing any sleeping Marines.

A better basketball player than a bass player, Krause also coordinated the construction of two concrete outdoor courts on Emirau. One wheelbarrow load of cement at a time from the Seabees supply ship, the courts took shape in an area cleared of the trees and coral that made up the terrain.

Krause's basketball skills had not diminished much. He had been a college All-American barely a decade earlier, and one of the country's most prominent professionals just three years before. "A Navy ship arrived and they had a team," says Colonel Norman R. Nickerson, Colonel Smith's successor as commanding officer, "but they were convincingly trounced by our squadron." Krause seldom found comparable competition among the Marines, but he relished the physical activity, running up and down the court, sweating in the tropical heat, forgetting for a few moments his loneliness and anxiety.

It probably reminded Krause of his childhood days in Davis Square Park, playing ball as long as the light—and his mother, no less stern than any colonel—allowed. Playing for the pure pleasure and escape of sport. Playing with the freestyle abandon impossible in organized competition, but welcome in the context of continuing combat. If Krause ever put his enduring belief that athletics help create and maintain a healthy body and mind to a laboratory test, it was on Emirau. It reinforced an idea he first heard Rockne articulate, that the nature of the competition did not matter—varsity or intramural, professional or recreational—as long as it engaged the body, mind and spirit in pursuit of a worthy objective.

"Those basketball courts," Ingberg says, "provided hours of fun and exercise for many of us." As the war wound down in the spring and summer of 1945, Krause helped organize many more sporting events for the Marines who waited, often for several idle months, to be rotated back to the States. Krause, in effect, became the athletic director of Emirau, years before Notre Dame recognized his knack for the job.

Krause organized daily football, basketball and baseball games, evening card games and entertainment in the officers' club. He even composed humorous memos in mock-military language.

One memo, entitled "Survival in America," aped the form of advice sent to Marines before they traveled to unfamiliar lands. After several months, or even years, in their primitive South Pacific surroundings, Krause figured they would find American customs as exotic as any foreign port where they spent their service. His memo informed returning Marines that "Most American cities and barrios have ordinances [that] may be inconvenient at times, but under all circumstances, Marine fliers should ask directions to the nearest 'toilet' [head] when the need is urgent." He added that, contrary to the culinary tastes developed in the mess halls, "America . . . suffers shortages of certain foods. It is difficult to obtain Spam at every meal. Neither milk nor eggs can be ordered in their familiar powdered form. Marine fliers frequently have been embarrassed by not having been checked out on the American custom of removing shells from boiled eggs. Do not mix soup and several courses, including dessert, in the same dish. Delicious as this may seem to you, Americans consider this a sign of inferior breeding. The country has limited supplies of canned foods. You may have to put up with fresh fruits, meats and vegetables until you return to the Pacific."

If they believed they could tolerate the strange and primitive American customs described, Krause composed another comic memo to help Marines compute the "points" they had accumulated toward a discharge. His "Point System, Discharge Thereof" informed Marines they needed one hundred points, gathered in any of the following ways, to return home:

(A) One (1) point for each four-year enlistment overseas.

(B) One (1) point for each participation in 5 major campaigns.

(C) One (1) point for each Purple Heart medal received.

(D) One (1) point for each group of ten (10) children.

(E) One (1) point for each lady friend. The term "lady friend" does not include gooks, spooks, or any other tropical or sub-tropical article.

(F) One (1) point may be awarded for participation in any of the following named engagements.

   1. The Boxer Rebellion

   2. Spanish American War

   3. Battle of Bull Run

   4. Boston Tea Party

   5. Engagements with the Tripoli Pirates.

A fortunate few could get a special dispensation, the memo explained: "Deceased persons may apply only in the event that proof is offered to the effect that the party in question has no special aptitude which can be utilized by the Marine Corps."

A bittersweet tone hovered over the humor. It hinted at the hardships soldiers faced and the reality that so many of their friends would never have the opportunity to return home, as Krause and his fellow Marines on Emirau were so anxious to do in the tedious months after the war. The laughter lightened the long days and reminded them how lucky they were. As pilot Hicks Smith says, "Ed Krause kept the spirits alive."

Golden Years

NOTRE DAME STOCKPILED FOOTBALL TALENT IN the years after World War II the way the Allies had accumulated ammunition. And the Irish triumphed as convincingly. Their roster resembled the credits of a contemporary war film. A leading man with matinee idol looks (Johnny Lujack); talented supporting players—one from rural Pennsylvania, the other from south Chicago—toiling selflessly for the good of the cause and ultimately honored for their valor (Leon Hart and George Connor); even a resident cutup who kept everyone laughing, often at inappropriate times (Zygmont Pierre Czarobski), a part John Candy could have given an endearing turn in a later era.

A legion of loyal athletes, physically and emotionally mature beyond their years, returned to Notre Dame with Leahy and Krause early in 1946. They picked up their lives where they left off, trying to rediscover the rhythms of ordinary living. Elise had kept the Krause family financially solvent during the war with a secretarial job in Chicago, where she and Eddie lived with her mother for the length of her husband's service. They returned to South Bend eager for a more normal lifestyle.

Eddie started school at St. Joseph's elementary in South Bend and the Krauses' second child, Mary, arrived with the first wave of the baby boom in 1946. Krause marveled at his good fortune. He had returned home to the wife he longed for on lonely nights overseas and a son anxious to learn the nuances of passing a football and shooting a basketball. A baby girl they named after Our Lady atop the Golden Dome arrived soon after. Notre Dame's staggering collection of football talent, perhaps its best since the Rockne era, only deepened his sense of satisfaction and anticipation for what the future might hold.

Leahy tempered his tenacious attitude somewhat to keep the war veterans on his roster from going AWOL, but he still expected perfection. And he would come remarkably close to achieving it. As Jack Connor notes in his account of the era, *Leahy's Lads*, "Never in collegiate history was there such an array of football talent on the college campuses. . . . Of all the great players and all the outstanding teams of that time, the Notre Dame teams were the best. Reflecting this, the four years, 1946–49, have been dubbed 'The Golden Era of Notre Dame Football.'" *Sports Illustrated* anointed those four teams the second best dynasty of the twentieth century, behind only the Boston Celtics teams that won eleven NBA championships from 1957 to '69. Stories abound about second- and third-string players who left Notre Dame with eligibility remaining, figuring they had a better chance for playing time in the pros.

With his fanatical determination, Leahy willed the Irish troops to victory. Whether out of fear or respect, or a combination of both, Leahy's subordinates followed his orders as if he were General Eisenhower himself. Late one night in the spring of 1946, not long after Krause returned from the war, he was in bed with the flu bordering on pneumonia when the phone rang after midnight. Elise crawled out of bed to answer it, telling the caller her husband was ill and could not come to the phone.

"Who is it?" Ed grumbled from the bed.

"I think his name is Leon Hart," Elise said. "He says he's at the South Bend train station."

Krause jumped up and grabbed the phone. "Leon, stay where you are," he wheezed in a voice barely above a whisper. "I'll be right down."

Hart could hear the commotion through the phone as Krause hurriedly fumbled through the darkness, pulling a topcoat over his pajamas and trying to explain to his wife what all the fuss was about.

"Where are you going?" Elise demanded.

"To the train station. I've got to pick him up."

"You'll die out there."

"It doesn't matter. If I don't get Hart on the team, Frank will kill me anyway."

If the returning veterans would form the foundation of Notre Dame's postwar football renaissance, Hart would become the cornerstone. Notre Dame had to have him, even if a sick coach had to venture out in the middle of the night to get him. Krause had corresponded with him previously, trying to sell the virtues of Notre Dame, one of several schools pursuing the Pennsylvania high school star. Hart had a certain fondness for Notre Dame, but he wanted to visit the school before making a commitment, somewhat unusual at a time when the Irish held a virtual monopoly on national popularity. It may have taken a few letters and a trip or two to a recruit's home, but the school essentially sold itself. Parents appreciated its academic reputation and strict social and religious codes, while athletes relished the media exposure and the chance to win championships. Recruiting visits had seldom been necessary at Notre Dame.

Hart's trip would be memorable for its clumsiness. Leahy had arranged it through Notre Dame alumnus Fritz Wilson, apparently without informing anyone else or making any reservations for the young man. Hesitant to call Leahy so late at night, Hart thumbed through the phone book for a listing for a "Krause, Edward," figuring an assistant would be somewhat more accommodating than the imposing Irish leader.

After absorbing his first impression of Notre Dame—this haggard, sick, sleep-deprived man they called Moose with a topcoat over his pajamas—Hart settled in for the night on a cot inside a transformed training room at the football stadium. Returning servicemen slept there until they found permanent places to stay. Not long after Hart had drifted off, one of those veterans—aspiring tackle and ex-Marine Theodore "Bull" Budynkiewicz—shook him awake, demanding Hart get out of his bed. With the speed and dexterity that would define his Heisman Trophy career, he did just that, wondering to himself why the Bull could not have used one of the other empty cots, but careful not to question him.

In the morning, still disoriented and uncertain about where he should be and when, Hart went hunting for some breakfast. He wandered into the athletic department, where a secretary gave him a meal pass, but still no Leahy and, you would think, no chance of Hart ever setting foot on that campus again. Except he kept thinking about that haggard, sick, sleep-deprived man they called Moose. That pneumonia-be-damned trip to the train station made an impression on Hart and, though he didn't realize it at the time, it served as a metaphor for Notre Dame football in the 1940s. Leahy, distant and distracted with the details of devising the perfect defensive tactic or offensive formation, delegated responsibility not only for recruiting, but also for relationships to his assistants. Irish players Pete Ashbaugh and Jim Mello once entertained their teammates with an interpretation of a typical conversation with Leahy on campus. When "The Master" bumped into his players away from the practice field, he always asked the same questions and paid no attention to the answers.

"Ah, James, how are you feeling?" Ashbaugh asked, mimicking Leahy's formal brogue.

"Not so good, Coach. I went to see the doctor last night and he thinks I might have a serious disease," Mello responded.

"That's fine, James, and how much do you weigh?"

"Because of the illness I've dropped 20 pounds."

"That's fine, lad, and how are your studies coming along?"

"Not good at all, Coach. I think I may be flunking all my courses."

"That's fine, James, and how are your folks?"

"Not very good. My mother passed away yesterday and my dad is seriously ill."

"Oh, that's fine, James. I'll see you on the practice field at 3:30."

Krause had his own problems keeping names straight during those revolving-door days. He called all the seniors "Sheriff," so when he bumped into them years later and said, "Hello, Sheriff," they would think he remembered them. Krause connected with the players on a much deeper level than Leahy. "He was the kind of guy, he was just such a people person, that you felt like you had a friend the first time you met him," Jack Connor says. "He was just that kind of guy."

At age thirty-three, Krause was not much older than many of the players he coached. Their lives all had been delayed and defined by war, creating a bond that extended far beyond the football field. Krause and the other Irish assistants served as seasoned peers, a buffer between the players and Leahy's biting sarcasm and uncompromising demands. Krause's easygoing personality was especially suited to that role, at that time. He served as an older-brother figure to many of the players in their mid-twenties. They respected Krause, but related to him more casually than they could Leahy. "He knew we could go out and have a few beers and not abuse things," says George Connor, Jack's older brother who transferred to Notre Dame after the war, finally uniting with Krause. "He'd go out and have a few beers with us. When he was coaching us, it was very intense, but we had a lot of fun, a lot of laughs. I probably worked harder for him than I would have for any other coach."

◆ ◆ ◆

As Notre Dame's head basketball coach, Krause had a similarly relaxed relationship with his players. He watched the final home games of the 1945–46 season after returning from the South Pacific, his confidence in the future growing with each convincing victory. Under Elmer Ripley, their second interim coach in two years, the Irish went 17-4 and spent six weeks as the No. 1 team in an informal Associated Press poll.

"With most of the Irish talent he was watching of undergraduate status, and some other previous monogrammers returning, Krause felt he was going to have some great years ahead," Tim Neely writes in *Hooping It Up: The Complete History of Notre Dame Basketball.* Considering the hard-luck history of the Irish on the hardwood, it should come as no surprise that it did not work out exactly that way. In fact, as college basketball developed unprecedented popularity over the next few years, the Irish program became indelibly identified as the scrappy underdog. "While Notre Dame was not generally one of the great teams in the nation at the time," Neely reports, "the Irish still fielded representative teams capable of a major upset now and then." That sentence essentially sums up the history of Notre Dame men's basketball.

Perhaps that underdog role was inevitable given the secondary status the basketball team had on its own campus. Even Krause, the head coach, focused on football first. Frenetic, freckled basketball assistant Red Foley ran practices and games until football season ended and Leahy set his staff free. "Red Foley was a little freckle-faced, red-haired guy and he had a tremendous knowledge of the Xs and Os," says Marty O'Connor, a player under Krause from 1948 to '51. "He spent his life studying film of offenses and defenses . . . and he had us in shape and understanding the offense we were running by the time Moose came aboard." After a month of preseason practice and two or three games under Foley, the basketball team had developed an identity and Krause seldom tinkered with it. He oversaw their productivity and performance like a CEO, occasionally demonstrating the proper rebounding technique with his ample backside or adding a variation to a standard play. Essentially, he served as a figurehead, relying on the ability and creativity of his players to produce results. "It's hard to describe the ease with which he approached his job," O'Connor says. "He was not trying to impress anybody with his coaching ability, but he could give you hell if you needed it."

Krause usually reserved his more volatile coaching techniques for the football field, and even then he used them sparingly. He coached such talented tackles during the 1946 season that Krause rarely raised his commanding voice. George Connor and Ziggy Czarobski, both war veterans and two of the best tackles ever to play at Notre Dame, had such ability and maturity that time-honored motivational techniques seemed unnecessary. Krause even relaxed on the full-contact drills Leahy expected his assistants to use as a firsthand evaluation tool. He did deliver an occasional message, lest the players mistake his leniency for a lack of authority.

One afternoon, amid the sound of grunts and groans and crashing pads inside the green fence surrounding Cartier Field, guards coach Joe McArdle, nursing a bum knee, asked Krause to work with Bill Fischer, the latest Irish lineman to assume the honorary nickname "Moose." With Leahy observing, Krause lined up across the imaginary line of scrimmage, face-to-face with Fischer. They dug their cleats into the turf for traction, anticipating the collision as McArdle called the signals.

"Set one! Hut!"

Instead of cheating on the count, as the coaches often did to create an advantage, Krause played it straight, allowing Fischer to hold his ground in the scrum in front of Leahy. Fischer even moved the bigger, stronger coach back a yard or two.

"Oh that-a-way, Bill Fischer," an impressed Leahy said. "Nice going, Bill Fischer."

When Leahy walked away, Krause turned to Fischer and said, "All right, one more time." They dug in as McArdle barked the signals again.

"Set one! Hut!"

This time, again without cheating the count, Notre Dame's original "Moose" reminded his namesake of the natural order of things.

"He *straightened* Fischer up. Marched him all the way to the green fence, pushed him all the way," Jack Connor says. "Banged him against the fence and with his forearm under his chin, he says, 'Just wanted to let you know who's boss.'"

His status thus reinforced, Krause dusted off his hands and returned to the tackles, the unit accused of having a tea party every afternoon during position drills because of the coach's easygoing disposition. The guards called McArdle, who ground them into hamburger on a daily basis, "Captain Bligh." The tackles had no such disparaging nicknames for Krause. Or for Fred Miller, for that matter, the Miller Brewing Company magnate and former All-American tackle at Notre Dame who frequently flew his private plane from Milwaukee to volunteer his wisdom to the team.

A fishing and hunting enthusiast and a major figure in the move of the Boston Braves to Milwaukee, Miller had a reputation as a sportsman as much as a businessman. He hired athletes to promote Miller Beer, making a regional brand popular nationwide. Miller's skill at the controls of a plane gave him the freedom to make frequent trips to his cabin in Canada and winter home in Miami Beach with his wife, Adele, and their nine children. Leahy, Krause and their families often accompanied them on these getaways, though Miller loved nothing more than visiting South Bend to assist the football team.

A close friend of all the coaches and a major benefactor to the university, Miller landed at the far end of Cartier Field in time for practice on many fall afternoons. He considered volunteer coaching as much a contribution to his alma mater as cutting a check. He was always willing to impart his wisdom, much to the delight of the weary tackles. George Connor and Ziggy Czarobski worked out an elaborate routine of questions for Miller about the minutiae of tackle play and he earnestly indulged them. "They played him like a violin," Jack Connor says.

"Coach Miller, in the game Saturday, this guy was playing on my outside shoulder and I wanted to take him in," Ziggie would begin, straight-faced. "Do I start out with my right foot?" After Miller's ten-minute demonstration and explanation, Krause would redirect the players' attention to the matter at hand, namely, "beating each other raw," as Leahy biographer Wells Twombly put it, "in order to demonstrate their love for the Mother of God."

"Wait a minute, Coach," George Connor would interject after a couple more repetitions, appearing quite confused. "When you do this technique, do you keep your thumbs this way or that way?"

"That's another ten minutes," Jack Connor says. "And Moose would just kind of roll his eyes. He'd kind of go along with it; he had to . . . Leahy'd go wild, but he couldn't do anything because Freddie Miller was his boy. We're down with the guards and we'd look up and say, 'Oh, look at this. The tackles. They're having a tea party again.'"

Leahy looked the other way, as he did to the players' occasional carousing, not only because war veterans like Connor and Czarobski were too old for traditional discipline. He tolerated the transparent questions and the "Muggers Club" meetings at Flytraps tavern because the 1946 team won with painstaking efficiency. They disciplined themselves like the adults they had become overseas, evident in the dissection of their first five opponents of the season.

With each victory the crescendo of anticipation built for the looming showdown with Army. First Illinois, then Pittsburgh, Purdue, Iowa and Navy fell to the extraordinarily talented Irish by a combined score of 177-12.

Newspapers published large-type hype as college football's most historic and competitive rivalry approached its climactic moment in Yankee Stadium on November 9, 1946. As college sports historian Murray Sperber writes in *Onward to Victory: The Crises That Shaped College Sports*, "The press proclaimed [it] 'the Football Battle of the Century'—the first time it had used this term." Even the august *New Yorker* covered the game, straying from its usual bias toward the Ivy League, setting the scene this way: "A sort of insanity seemed to seize the city last weekend . . ."

Notre Dame students wore "SPATNC" pins on their lapels—that is, "Society for the Prevention of Army's Third National Championship." New York Central trains overflowed with fans heading east. Tickets, sold out since July, went for as much as $200 outside the stadium, dismaying administrators of both schools already concerned that scalping, gambling and boorish fan behavior threatened the integrity of the rivalry.

Leahy and Army's Red Blaik had, at best, a grudging respect for each other, adding a simmering undercurrent to this heated renewal of hostilities. Notre Dame carried a grudge from the two previous lopsided defeats, even though most of the current players had not participated. Army aimed to assert its superiority against an Irish team at full strength for the first time since three consecutive shutouts of the Cadets from 1941 to '43.

"All right, lads," Leahy said in the Notre Dame locker room moments before the game, igniting Irish intensity after a week—no, make that three years—of restless anticipation with six words.

"Army's out there waiting for you."

They ran out of the locker room and into a brick wall, giving no ground themselves in a 0-0 tie derided as tedious by many at the time, but a classic from a historical perspective. On a field full of Heisman Trophy winners and Hall of Famers, aggressive defense strangled conservative offense. "All-America backs were merely members of the supporting cast," the *Chicago Tribune* reported. "The real actors were up front along the scrimmage strip. It was there that plays perished."

Johnny Lujack, whose tender ankle worried subway alumni from coast-to-coast (the *New York Times* even published a picture of trainer Hugh Burns taping it before a practice session), helped preserve the tie under risky conditions. When Doc Blanchard darted around the Notre Dame defense, apparently headed for a touchdown, Lujack's diving tackle truncated his run. That play defined the game and perhaps the era. Notre Dame's star quarterback, also playing defense in the custom of the time, leaped off an injured ankle to detour a potential touchdown. For all the talent on the field that day, Army-Notre Dame 1946 stands as a competition between two institutions, two teams, a tribute to "the everlasting team work of every bloomin' soul," as the *Chicago Tribune* described it.

Still, it stung. Losing would have been more devastating, but at least it would have been conclusive. More than hard to swallow, a tie seemed indigestible. Krause, along with fellow assistant Bernie Crimmins and Irish scout Jack Lavalle, remained in their press box perch for thirty minutes after the game, reviewing the frustrating scenarios. When they finally made their way to the locker room, they joined Leahy and McArdle to pick over the details some more, as if the game film flickered in front of them. By the time the coaches finished their mental replay, the team had long since returned to their hotel, so they shuffled out of a darkened Yankee Stadium and hailed a cab for the ride back to Manhattan.

✦ ✦ ✦

Leahy worked himself sick. Days preoccupied with preparation and apprehension for the next opponent and nights spent sleeping on a cot in his office, if at all, finally took a toll. After a rout of Northwestern in a cold rain the week after the Army tie, Leahy fell ill with the flu, laryngitis and a recurrence of the spinal arthritis condition that had sent him to the Mayo Clinic in 1942. Doctors ordered him to remain home in bed the week before the final game of the season against Southern California.

Krause became the acting head coach in Leahy's absence. In the slanting shadows and bitter chill of late November, he put the Irish through their usual meticulous preparation. Without the authoritarian presence of Leahy, practices were much more relaxed. Businesslike and efficient, Notre Dame studied new nuances in the game plan and performed its daily drills even without the coach's relentless prodding.

Leahy's spirit still inhabited the practice field, albeit in jest. Late Thursday afternoon, during the final full practice before Saturday's season finale, Krause put the offensive starters through a noncontact scrimmage with a group of reserves. At the other end of Cartier Field, the second-team offense did the same, repeatedly running familiar plays, just to refine the timing. As the first-team broke from their huddle before one play, George Connor spotted something in the distance and abruptly stopped his trot to the line of scrimmage.

"Look at that," he said, gesturing toward the reserves. "Look at them."

Everybody looked in that direction to discover the second-team offense running backwards, like a rewinding play on a game film. They returned to their original positions and ran the play over again, stopping in unison, as if a projectionist had flipped a switch, then backtracking to their previous formation. From forty yards away in the hazy darkness, the scene took on the sepia tone of the grainy films Leahy dissected every week in team meetings.

Krause played the part of Leahy the film critic, allowing the play to develop in the distance and then hollering, "Run that play over again!" Every player who made a mistake on those celluloid reruns dreaded hearing Leahy say that in a team meeting, but Krause's imitation only enhanced the amusement. Their precision amazed him, proving what many observers had suspected—this team literally learned its plays backward and forward.

"Marvelous, marvelous," Krause laughed.

That word also summarizes the 1946 season. Marvelous. A 26-6 win to end the season at home against Southern California, combined with Army's narrow victory over Navy, earned Notre Dame another national championship.

✦ ✦ ✦

Notre Dame's 1946–47 basketball team, already 2-0 by the time Krause arrived, looked nothing like the team he saw at the end of the previous season. Leo Klier had graduated with his class despite a remaining year of eligibility. Ray Corley and Tom O'Keefe returned to Georgetown with their coach, Elmer Ripley. And Johnny Dee went back to Loyola.

That left the Irish with a youthful, but still talented, lineup. Sophomores John Brennan, Leo Barnhorst, Paul Gordon and Jim O'Halloran logged most of the minutes, along with a freshman considered the future of the program—Kevin O'Shea. On rickety knees, O'Shea led the Irish to their first twenty-win season in nine years.

In a harbinger of his future, O'Shea became a second-team All-American as a freshman, but nagging knee problems tempered his talent. "Kevin O'Shea, in my mind, is very similar to Mickey Mantle," Barnhorst says. "There's no telling how good he would have been if he had good legs."

He was good enough to lead Notre Dame to an 11-2 start and a No. 3 national ranking. A showdown with No. 1 Kentucky loomed in Louisville, but the team of Adolph Rupp and future Olympians Ralph Beard and Alex Groza knocked the Irish off their pedestal, 60-30. While Notre Dame regrouped to complete the season with a 20-4 record, fueling hopeful speculation that the administration might end its postseason ban, the year ended typically for the Irish—successfully, but with lingering questions about what might have been.

Notre Dame fans at least had reason for hope. A team so young, orbiting around a star like O'Shea, had to feel confident about the future. As Krause turned his attention to spring football in 1947, he maintained high hopes for his basketball program.

Leahy had designs on a dynasty as the 1947 football season approached, but he feared his players indulged too much in the spoils of their success. George Connor and Ziggie Czarobski, the tackles who knew all the angles on the field and off, spent the summer in Lake Delavan, Wisconsin. Ziggie worked as a bouncer at a bar, spending his days on the beach sipping a few beers and enjoying the scenery of sand, surf and skimpy swimsuits. Connor found a job with Notre Dame alumnus Ray Morrissey, who needed construction work done on his private lake in the area. Morrissey allowed Connor to slip away most afternoons to join Ziggie on the beach. As Jack Connor put it in *Leahy's Lads*, "Nobody ever accused Moose Krause's tackles of being dumb."

Nobody ever accused Leahy of being deaf and blind, either, and news of Ziggie's ballooning weight reached South Bend. In early August, Ziggie received a telegram:

Mr. Zygmont Czarobski:

Understand you weigh 275 pounds. You could make All-American next season if you were in proper condition. You must report for summer practice at 225 pounds or you will not play for the University of Notre Dame this fall. I do not want any funny fat men on my team.

Frank Leahy

Leahy sent a copy to Connor, a captain for the 1947 season, to reinforce his seriousness. Ziggie spent the final three weeks of his summer vacation on a crash diet, exercising every night with Connor. He still reported twenty-five pounds overweight and trembling at the thought of facing Leahy. Ziggie begged for an extension from Leahy, no dummy either, who granted it to avoid cutting one of his best players.

"Zygmont," Leahy intoned, "I will give you two more weeks to make your weight and not one moment more."

After two more weeks of intense workouts, in addition to two-a-day practice sessions in oppressive heat, Ziggie "looked like an ad for Charles Atlas," Jack Connor says. But he tipped the scales at 232 pounds, seven over the Leahy-imposed limit. Always quick to devise a way around the rules, Ziggie slipped stadium caretaker Joe Dierickx ten dollars to manipulate the scale to come up eight pounds light. Leahy never even looked at the scale, though, taking Ziggie at his word that he was down to 224 pounds. Leahy knew he could not afford to lose a star tackle, and a month of intense workouts had left Ziggie in perhaps the best condition of his career. The coach had made his point.

With most of the first and second string returning from the previous year, the 1947 Irish football team looked familiar and, like Ziggie, more fine-tuned than before. Even Leahy felt the emphasis on fundamentals could be sacrificed with this team in favor of simple timing and tactical details. One day during preseason practice, George Connor told Chicago sportswriter Warren Brown that he and his teammates felt apprehensive about the de-emphasis of the principles of blocking and tackling and footwork. He feared they were becoming sloppy, in danger of devolving into "just another football team." Brown related this to Leahy, who apologized at the next team meeting and pledged to return to the basics. To prove it, he reached beneath his podium and produced an oblong, leather object. "Lads," he said, "this is a football."

"Coach, wait a minute," Ziggie piped in from his front-row seat. "I'm trying to take notes. You're going too fast."

✦ ✦ ✦

Leahy's rigorous, regimented practices and daily meetings were so challenging the players should have received credit hours. Their shared experience forged a bond among the Irish akin to wartime camaraderie. "When you played for him it was like going to war," Jack Connor says. "Just like the guys in the service that were on a ship together or on Guadalcanal together, you felt like you went through a war together because it was so hard."

Leahy's lieutenants, among them Krause, McArdle, Crimmins and Wally Ziemba, endured their own physical and mental wounds working for him. First of all, they battled their own players in live blocking and tackling drills—without pads, or even gloves and stocking caps on cold days—to establish their toughness. They were still in their physical prime, all former players with size, strength and savvy enough to deliver more punishment than they absorbed.

None had Leahy's meticulous, tireless nature. Every day after practice, he gathered his assistants for an evaluation of every player on the roster, poring over every nuance of their development, from tactical aptitude to mental attitude. "Frank wanted to know everything," Krause said.

When they got a brief break for dinner, Krause hustled home to see Elise, Eddie and Mary, but he would be expected back at the office before long. The coaches often studied game film or just talked football long into the night—usually longer than Krause cared to be there. Everybody would be asleep by the time he returned home, though occasionally Elise would stir and wonder where he had been so late. "I'd say, 'Football practice, honey. Go back to sleep,'" Krause said in *Notre Dame's Greatest Coaches*. "She couldn't believe it. And sometimes I couldn't either."

Leahy's relentless approach produced perfection in 1947. Only Purdue and Northwestern came within two touchdowns of the Irish. A rematch against Army, the last in the venerable series for many years because of the surrounding unseemliness, ended 27-7 in favor of Notre Dame.

By November, the Irish were playing so well that Leahy left the team to Krause for the home finale against Tulane, so he could personally scout feared rival Southern California. A 59-6 rout of Tulane—the most points ever for a Leahy team—gave Krause a perfect 2-0 record as Notre Dame's acting head coach. The only perfect coaching record in school history, he often boasted.

Leahy's advance work paid off two weeks later in Los Angeles. The Irish rolled to a 38-7 win, polishing off a perfect 9-0 record and a third straight national title with Leahy at the helm (1943, '46 and '47). Everybody planned to celebrate. Leahy invited the assistants to his hotel room, where he poured each a glass of scotch to toast the championship. After their drink, as the assistants planned to scatter to meet friends and family for a night on the town, Leahy reached for a pad and pen. "Now," he said, "let's start planning for next year."

"We looked at each other in disbelief," Ziemba said in *Leahy's Lads*. "Here we had just finished the last game of a long season with a great victory that meant we had won back-to-back national championships, and Coach Leahy wanted to get to work on next year—unbelievable.

"Somehow we managed some excuses and did go out and celebrate."

✦ ✦ ✦

Krause gave up his football duties after the 1947 season to assume more administrative responsibilities and allow more time for himself and his growing family. He continued as head basketball coach and became Leahy's assistant athletic director, still the work of two men, but a welcome relief from his previous schedule. Leahy delegated more and more administrative work, leaving Krause to tend to the details of facilities and scheduling that distracted the coach from football. Coaching basketball also demanded extensive time and travel, but Krause had a much more normal life without his football responsibilities.

Krause's personality blended well into the athletic administration offices in the basement of Breen-Phillips Hall, a dormitory on campus. Business manager Bob Cahill and sports information director Charlie Callahan shared the Spartan space with Krause. Their plain wooden desks butted up against each other, and together they handled the daily details of Notre Dame athletics like a family business.

Eleanor VanDerHagen served as Krause's secretary from his first day as an athletic administrator. Their lives became intertwined with the rest of the department's families. Lasting friendships formed, making for a vibrant working atmosphere and even livelier parties.

Fall, in particular, became a social season. Cocktail parties and pep rallies and ceremonial presentations filled football weekends, often culminating with dinner and drinks at Krause's home. It became the social epicenter of Notre Dame's annual fall football pageants. Dignitaries from all walks of life joined representatives of the visiting team and friends from South Bend for gatherings that often became boisterous celebrations no matter the outcome of the game.

They entertained celebrities like Pat O'Brien, who starred in *Knute Rockne, All-American* and always shared a bottle of scotch and a conversation with Krause when their paths crossed in New York or Los

Angeles. Comedian and football aficionado Bob Hope also visited several times over the years and became an occasional golfing partner of Krause's. Sporting characters like Philadelphia Eagles owner Leonard Tose and the Oakland A's Charley O. Finley frequented the parties.

For all the celebrities who passed through town one week or another and gravitated toward Krause's home, a steady stream of friends and family were the regulars. "You couldn't get in, there were so many people," Elise's sister Dorothy Feeney says.

They somehow found room for everyone, even the occasional stranger. Ella Mattocks, a Notre Dame fan from Jamestown, New York, cobbled together whatever extra money she could for a bus trip to a game every year. One year, she coincidentally met Eddie Krause selling programs on campus and they struck up a conversation. He invited her over and she became a friend and frequent houseguest of the Krauses for years to come.

Courteous and meticulous, Elise Krause organized these affairs down to the smallest details. They called her the Pearl Mesta of Notre Dame. "Mrs. Krause was the most gracious, beautiful wife that anybody could have wanted," VanDerHagen says.

"She was very good for Ed," Dorothy Feeney says. "She knew how to do everything around the house. He didn't know what a screw was. She was his backbone really, I think. She was the woman behind the man."

Krause agreed. He often told a joke, typical of the time, but especially resonant as it applied to their relationship. "When we got married, I told my wife I would make all the big decisions and she would make all the small decisions," Krause would say. "So far, there have been no big decisions." He told that story to emphasize Elise's dominant role around the house, but it also hinted at the twinges of guilt he felt at how often his job kept him away from home.

Always one of the most popular people in college athletics, Krause became an ambassador for Notre Dame, a genial presence to dull the sting of the losses Leahy inflicted. Krause clinked glasses, shook hands and told jokes, creating immeasurable goodwill for a university often perceived as arrogant, especially with the mercurial Leahy as its most prominent public figure.

Krause's way with people inspired several job opportunities over the years, usually at a substantial increase in salary and power. Tose offered him the general manager's position with the Philadelphia Eagles. Finley made similar overtures to woo him to the Oakland A's front office. Fred Miller even made Krause a standing offer to become a vice president of his expanding brewing company. He never considered leaving Notre Dame. No job could have been as fulfilling to him.

Among alumni and other friends of Notre Dame, Krause's connection to the Rockne legend and his insider status on the campus athletic scene made him a modern icon. A coveted and accomplished banquet speaker, he often spent weeks on the road sprinkling wit and wisdom among Notre Dame's true believers. Krause's willingness to accommodate requests for tickets and impositions on his time endeared him to people far beyond the university community. He often delayed his departure to his next destination to speak at a Communion breakfast or visit an ailing Irish fan in the hospital because an acquaintance asked. From Norfolk to Albuquerque, he delivered the gospel of Notre Dame football to fans far removed from the Golden Dome, often at great personal sacrifice. "To say that the men of the Holy Name Society of Nativity Church and our honored guests at the Mother's Day Communion Breakfast were thrilled by your presence amongst them and your delightful talk is putting it exceedingly mildly," E.L. Collins of Scranton, Pennsylvania, wrote to Krause after one such event. "I am especially grateful to you because I realize you fitted this engagement into an already overcrowded schedule and because you sacrificed the pleasure of being with your wife and family on Mother's Day to do it."

Edward Walter Krauciunas in 1926 before growing to the size that would earn him the nickname "Moose." His high school football coach, Norm Barry, who bestowed the nickname, also shortened Krauciunas's hard-to-pronounce last name to "Krause" on the practice field. As a judge in Chicago, Barry later made the change official in the eyes of the law. *(Krause family photo.)*

DeLaSalle Institute's 1929 National Catholic Interscholastic Champions, featuring Ed Krause, third from the right in the front row, and his brother, Phil, seated at far right. *(Krause family photo.)*

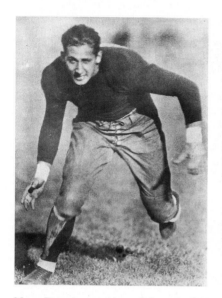

Notre Dame's star athlete of the early 1930s, Krause possessed a combination of size and agility uncommon in that era, making him a dominant tackle in football and a high-scoring center in basketball. *(Football: Krause family photo. Basketball: University of Notre Dame Archives.)*

After graduating from Notre Dame, Krause turned down a lucrative offer to play professional football for the Chicago Bears to be athletic director and coach of all sports at Saint Mary's University in Winona, Minnesota. Here, Krause imparts the finer points of football to Saint Mary's 1934 team captain Al Teske. *(Krause family photo.)*

With a delegation of Lithuanian-American athletes from Chicago, Krause traveled to his ancestral country in 1935 to train citizens of Lithuania in a variety of sports. Traveling overseas in first-class accommodations gave Krause ample time to lounge in the sun. *(Krause family photo.)*

Krause with his bride-to-be Elizabeth Linden in 1937. Elise, as her friends called her, visited Krause once a month in Minnesota and he passed through Chicago from time to time as a semipro basketball player, their only opportunities to spend time together during a four-year courtship. They were married in 1938. *(Krause family photo.)*

Krause watches as coaching legend Frank Leahy diagrams the tactics the Notre Dame football team will use against its opponents. Krause returned to his alma mater as an assistant in 1942, his easygoing demeanor a welcome complement to Leahy's relentless style. *(Krause family photo.)*

Training as a Marine intelligence officer, Krause faced an uncertain future in the South Pacific. Leaving his wife and young son behind agonized him, but Krause considered it his duty—and a necessity to maintain respect among the returning servicemen he would coach at Notre Dame. *(Krause family photo.)*

Krause and Rev. James Gannon, the Marine Corps chaplain on Emirau, became close friends during their service. They shared many spiritual experiences that formed their lasting bond, from baptisms to weddings among the native people to a burial of a group of fallen Marines. Krause joked that he spent so much time with Gannon because the chaplain had the only cold beer on the island. *(Krause family photo.)*

Antoun, center, a leader among the native Moro people on the island of Emirau, where Krause served during World War II, provided valuable assistance to the Marines in the region. Krause became close friends with Antoun, who had been trained by Catholic missionaries before the war, and helped foster his interest in the priesthood. *(Krause family photo.)*

Krause gives some final pointers to his starting five, from left, Leroy Leslie, Jim Gibbons, Marty O'Connor, Dan Bagley, and Norbert Lewinski, before his last game as Notre Dame's head basketball coach in 1951. *(Acme Photo.)*

Frank Leahy presented Krause with a combination briefcase-overnight bag in a ceremony before his final game as head basketball coach. That token of appreciation hinted at the work that lay ahead for Krause as Notre Dame's first full-time athletic director, a job that would demand extensive travel as a representative of the university. *(South Bend Tribune photo.)*

Notre Dame basketball's centers of attention: Krause, center, flanked by two of the players who followed in his footsteps as star Irish centers: Paul Nowak, left, and Dick Rosenthal, who became Notre Dame athletic director in the 1980s. *(South Bend Tribune photo.)*

Ed and Elise Krause with their three children in 1963: Mary; Edward Jr., who was studying to be a priest; and Phil, the rambunctious youngster. *(Krause family photo.)*

Gracious and gregarious hosts, Ed and Elise Krause entertained dozens of Notre Dame fans, from celebrities to "subway alumni," every football weekend. *(Krause family photo.)*

On a trip to Italy for Edward Jr.'s ordination as a Holy Cross priest in 1966, the Krause family traveled the countryside together. Krause had once considered becoming a priest, and his son's pursuit of the vocation thrilled him and Elise, who would suffer debilitating injuries in a car accident just weeks after returning from Rome. *(Krause family photo.)*

Mary Krause's wedding to Sandy Carrigan was one of the Krause family's most uplifting moments in the years after the car accident that left Elise brain damaged and frail. *(Krause family photo.)*

Elise Krause managed to summon the strength to attend special functions, like Krause's induction into the National Basketball Hall of Fame in 1976. *(Krause family photo.)*

Krause had a sense of comic timing that entertained audiences around the world and even cracked up comedian and football aficionado Bob Hope, a friend and occasional golfing partner. *(Krause family photo.)*

Krause worked closely for thirty years with Notre Dame's executive vice president, Rev. Edmund P. Joyce, the chairman of the faculty board in control of athletics. *(Krause family photo.)*

Krause cherished his lifelong friendships with the close-knit "Leahy's Lads," including this talented and gregarious pair of tackles who formed the foundation of Notre Dame's success in the 1940s, Zygmont Pierre "Ziggie" Czarboski, left, and George Connor. *(Krause family photo.)*

A retirement roast became a toast to Krause, who nevertheless kept the irreverent spirit of the evening alive for months with a "lawsuit" for defamation of character against his close friends at the head table. *(Krause family photo.)*

Among the gifts bestowed on Krause at the time of his retirement, a Cadillac which wore a path to the South Bend Country Club, where he received a lifetime membership, and soon reeked of cigars from the lifetime supply he received. *(Krause family photo.)*

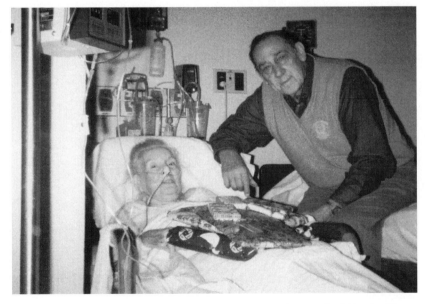

In retirement, Krause spent most of his time at Elise's bedside at Cardinal Nursing Home, feeding her meals, singing her songs, and bringing her gifts, as he did on Christmas morning in 1988. *(Krause family photo.)*

Krause had a bond with legendary Notre Dame coach Ara Parseghian and his wife, Katie, that transcended a typical working relationship. "Even as volatile as I was," Parseghian says, "we never had an argument. That was a tribute to him, not me." *(Krause family photo.)*

President Ronald Reagan, who played George Gipp in *Knute Rockne All-American*, traveled to Notre Dame in 1988 to dedicate the new Rockne postage stamp. Krause's brief speech included one of the ceremony's most memorable lines: "Never in our wildest dreams," Krause said, "did we think George Gipp would become President of the United States." *(Krause family photo.)*

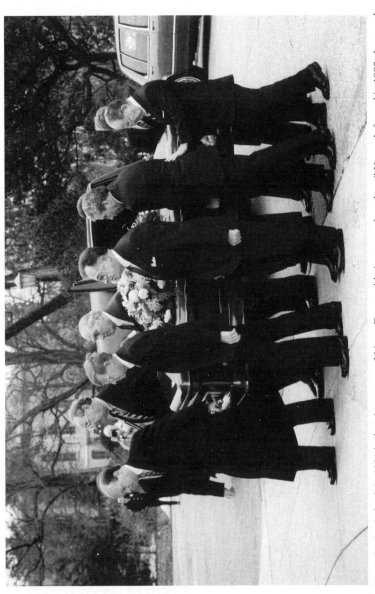

Not since Knute Rockne's death in 1931 had such an array of Notre Dame athletic stars gathered until Krause's funeral in 1992. Among the pallbearers were athletic director Dick Rosenthal, football coach Lou Holtz, former All-American tackle George Connor, coach and athletic administrator George Kelly, and basketball coach John MacLeod. *(South Bend Tribune photo/ED BAILOTTS.)*

Edward "Moose" Krause, 1913-1992. *(Gary Mills photo.)*

Krause became synonymous with Notre Dame, the gregarious and generous personality he inherited from his father providing valuable public relations and speeding his ascension within the administration. "It is an open secret that [Krause] will eventually become athletic director," sports columnist and Notre Dame graduate Red Smith wrote in the *New York Herald Tribune* when Krause became Leahy's assistant athletic director. "The plan appears to have a twofold purpose. One is to take some of the load off the master, to leave him free to devote all his attention to the job he does as well as any one alive and much better than most. The job, that is, of teaching young men to mangle one another in massed formation.

"The other purpose is to cash in on big, amiable Moose Krause's personal popularity. It is often said that whereas Knute Rockne could wallop opponents and make 'em like it, Leahy lacks his gift for salving a victim's wounds. . . . In the future, apparently, Leahy will dish out the medicine while Moose assures the patient that it's syrup he's swallowing."

Despite his easygoing demeanor, Krause's competitive fire burned during basketball season, revealing itself in subconscious ways. "He must play the games in his sleep at night as he jumps, twitches, turns, calls out, and tosses all over his bed," Elise wrote in an essay about the life of a coach's wife. "In the morning I doubt he feels he has hit the pillow."

Krause seldom appeared so agitated during his waking hours. He approached coaching basketball with all the outward intensity of an after-dinner speech—and he reserved most of his verbosity for the dais. In *The Catholic Universe Bulletin*, Fred McCool wrote that Krause "gave the 'bull' tag to the popular conception of pre-game pep talks designed to foment a do-or-die enthusiasm in cagers . . . he has the briefest and most effective pep talk in the game. It's a good, solid, down-to-earth American word—'Shoot.'"

Only rebounding—or rather, the lack of it—could raise Krause's ire. With his still-agile frame, he demonstrated the fundamentals to his big men often, expecting them to execute this essential skill in game situations. When they failed, Krause let them hear about it.

"I'll never forget one night in Chicago Stadium, we were playing DePaul, and our locker room was where the Blackhawks hockey team dressed," Marty O'Connor says. "The ceiling was maybe seven or eight feet high, it was just a box down there. Well, he was laying into somebody and put his arms out and leaped up, trying to show us how to rebound, and he hit his head on the ceiling. Damn near knocked him out."

Even Krause's rare reprimands were delivered with a humorous chaser, and not always of the accidental physical-comedy variety. Trainer Hugh Burns, fortunately nearby for occasions like the collision with the ceiling at Chicago Stadium, often mimicked Krause's facial expressions during his lectures, leaving the players struggling to stifle their laughter.

Krause did not mind levity accompanying his lessons. He believed more could be achieved through a patient approach to teaching the game. "He wasn't the hell and brimstone or win-one-for-the-Gipper type. He was a mild-mannered man by nature and each year he mellowed more," O'Connor says. "I think he realized that you could accomplish more with soft talk than yelling and screaming."

Some of Notre Dame's greatest basketball accomplishments of the postwar era could be attributed to the yelling and screaming of fans in the claustrophobic Fieldhouse. The G.I. Bill swelled Notre Dame's (all male) enrollment and overflowed the Fieldhouse with 5,000 excitable students, often leaving no tickets available for the general public. It became so difficult for opposing teams that Krause began to have trouble scheduling home games against major programs.

On February 2, 1948—Krause's thirty-fifth birthday—No. 1 Kentucky visited, its contract signed before the Fieldhouse took on such a feverish atmosphere. Notre Dame carried a thirty-seven-game home win streak into the game. With five players who would win a gold medal in the 1948 Olympics, though, Kentucky appeared capable of intimidating the young

Irish into submission. Legendary "Baron" Adolph Rupp had built one of the best college basketball teams ever, virtually the same group that had beaten Notre Dame by 30 the year before in Louisville.

Rupp had not anticipated the offense Krause installed to draw tall Kentucky stars Ralph Beard and Alex Groza away from the basket and clear the baseline for Kevin O'Shea. Krause stationed big men Leo Barnhorst and John Foley at the foul line, forcing Beard and Groza to step out to defend them. That left O'Shea open to maneuver around the basket for 25 points, fouling out two Kentucky players in the process. "Rupp had never seen this 'high-post' setup before," Tim Neely writes in *Hooping It Up: The Complete History of Notre Dame Basketball.* "Soon after this night, he adopted it himself and used it the rest of his career."

Rupp also had never seen an atmosphere quite like he encountered in the Fieldhouse. Students squeezed into the sweaty little bandbox and squalled. Kentucky's bench, coincidentally enough, was just a few feet from the Notre Dame pep band's perch, all the better to give Rupp's timeout speeches a musical accompaniment. And a few hundred black-robed priests occupied the seats directly across from their bench, as if to inform the Wildcats that Notre Dame did indeed have a prayer.

In that intimidating atmosphere, the Irish set off a raucous celebration with a 64-55 win. Rupp fumed about the conditions, vowing never to bring Kentucky back to the Fieldhouse after his fifth loss without a win in its disorienting confines.

That victory raised anew the nagging question—what might have been?—in the middle of another modest season. Notre Dame had lost four games before knocking off Kentucky, essentially falling from the national elite. Defeating the Wildcats revived some interest, but the Irish then lost three of their next six.

A trip to New York in the middle of a five-game win streak to end the season stirred the optimism once again. New York University, 19-0 and ranked No. 1 since Kentucky's defeat, awaited at Madison Square

Garden, a marquee game in a burgeoning sport as the season approached its climax.

Notre Dame practiced at the Garden in front of 2,000 interested onlookers the morning of the game. Leo Barnhorst, one of the Irish leaders, burst a blood vessel in his ankle during the workout. Trainer Hugh Burns hustled him back to the Commodore Hotel, where he quickly ordered a bucket of ice for the ankle and two shots of Canadian Club.

"Hughie, I'm not going to drink two shots of Canadian Club," Barnhorst said.

"No, I want you to drink one," Burns said, "and I don't want you to drink alone."

As Barnhorst nursed his ankle and his drink in the afternoon, the phone rang in his room. It was the owner of an Italian restaurant in South Bend where the team often gathered. He had heard about Barnhorst's ankle and wondered about his status for the game that night. "I didn't know this at the time," Barnhorst says. "He was a gambler. He bet on games."

So, it seemed, were many of those 2,000 "fans" at practice. They craved inside information, and Barnhorst's ankle injury could have had a dramatic impact on Notre Dame's chances. Word spread quickly.

"Are you going to play?" the restaurant owner from Indiana asked.

"I don't know," Barnhorst said. "I really don't know."

"Well, I just wanted to wish you well," he said, innocently enough, and Barnhorst never gave it another thought.

Gambling was becoming an epidemic in college basketball, reaching all the way to point-shaving players at some high-profile programs, but the scandal would not make national news until 1951. It remained little more than a rumor, especially to Irish players isolated from its insidious effects by geography and the austerity of campus life. "We knew it went on, but . . . at Notre Dame we led a pretty cloistered life," Barnhorst says.

They won and lost honestly, although with a six-point deficit at half-time against NYU, Krause questioned their effort. He did it without words, letting the team stew at their lockers in silence—"he was really pulling a Rockne," Barnhorst says—until a knock at the door told them it was time to return to the floor. Krause stood up, looked around the room and said with disgust, "I never thought I'd see a Notre Dame team that would quit."

"God damn, we tore out of that locker room," Barnhorst says. "He pulled a Rockne that night." With Barnhorst holding NYU star Dolph Schayes to eight points despite his swollen ankle, the Irish performed a stirring comeback to defeat another No. 1 team.

Krause beamed all the way back to South Bend. "I've never seen the man happier," O'Connor says. "He was just elated after that game."

No sooner had Krause arrived back home and guided the team through the final two weeks of a 17-7 season than he hit the road again in an administrative capacity to raise awareness and money for Notre Dame athletics. Leahy, still the athletic director, had spring football practice to fret about, no longer a concern for Krause, who was becoming a roving ambassador for the university.

Capitalizing on his popularity among alumni and fellow athletic administrators, Notre Dame made Krause more and more visible as a speaker and a representative at meetings and conventions. He exuded an endearing combination of pride and humility that impressed virtually everyone whose path he crossed. Broad-shouldered and dapper, with his thinning brown hair combed straight back to reveal a wide, welcoming face, Krause cut an impressive figure. His charisma captivated a room; his genuine friendliness warmed it. "The perfect Rotarian," *Chicago Tribune* sports columnist Dave Condon wrote, "to salve egos galled by The Master."

Leahy occasionally galled even his own bosses with his single-minded pursuit of victory. When university president Rev. John Cavanaugh appointed Rev. Theodore Hesburgh executive vice president in 1949, he charged him with reorganizing the athletic department. "The biggest problem was Leahy himself, who had become so powerful that he did whatever he pleased, running what amounted to an autonomous fief-dom," Michael O'Brien writes in *Hesburgh: A Biography*.

Leahy and Hesburgh clashed over the seemingly trivial matter of the number of players on the travel roster for a game against the University of Washington. It was the culmination of several months of tension after Hesburgh had instituted new guidelines for the athletic department. Elevated to athletic director on March 22, 1949, Krause worked with Hesburgh to develop those rules. They placed limits on complimentary tickets and gave team doctors ultimate authority in determining the extent of injuries in addition to reducing the number of players allowed to travel from forty-four to thirty-eight.

Powerful on campus and popular among influential alumni, Leahy represented a problem for Hesburgh. He sought Cavanaugh's support in the battle over the travel roster, which Leahy submitted with the same number he took in previous years.

"We're at a crossroads," Hesburgh told Cavanaugh, according to O'Brien, "and if he doesn't comply, either he goes or I go."

"Very simple," Cavanaugh said. "What you propose is the right thing to do. Either he complies, or he goes."

With Krause serving as a liaison between the two, Leahy ultimately complied and his relationship with Hesburgh warmed somewhat in the ensuing years, the administration's ultimate control of all athletic matters firmly established.

◆ ◆ ◆

With the football team commanding most of the attention on campus, Krause's basketball team embarked on a rugged schedule for the 1948–49 season. A talented roster of experienced players, most notably the sensa-tional Kevin O'Shea, inspired Krause to accept several invitations for high-profile road games. That left no room for the usual litany of lambs to the slaughter at the beginning of the season that helped pad the Irish record in the past. Travel fatigue, talented opposition and O'Shea's nagging injuries diminished the preseason enthusiasm and the Irish finished 17-7.

Notre Dame lost an overtime game to Illinois for its first season-opening defeat in twenty-five years. DePaul defeated the Irish 58-39 at the Fieldhouse, their worst home loss in a decade. Kentucky repaid Notre Dame for the previous season's upset with a 62-38 thrashing in Louisville, a game cited among those with Wildcat players suspected of being on the take in the point-shaving scandal exposed two years later.

As rumors swirled about gamblers infiltrating college sports, Krause took steps to assure it did not taint his team. He summoned every player to his office individually, asking them directly if gamblers had ever approached them and insisting they tell him immediately if it ever happened in the future. "We'll protect you and get the authorities in and make sure it's resolved," he assured them.

Kevin O'Shea returned for the 1949–50 season, finally healthy and ready to realize the potential he had flashed through the frustrating starts and stops of the previous two years. He rewrote the record books, becoming the first Irish player to score 1,000 career points and setting the single-season standard, but he had little support.

When the season began, three starters had never played a varsity minute and their inexperience showed in a 15-9 season that reached its peak in January with another upset of Kentucky. "Now the big gun for the Ruppians was seven-foot center Bill Spivey, who was perfect for the high-post offense which 'The Baron' had adopted after ND had used it on him two years earlier," Neely writes in *Hooping It Up*.

Krause adopted a defensive tactic that had been used against him as a player—he concentrated on stifling Spivey's teammates, rather than trying to stop the seven-footer. Spivey scored 27 points, but the rest of the Wildcats were ineffective in a 64-51 loss to the Irish.

A loss later in the year at St. Louis yielded a victory for the Irish. Krause met Dick Rosenthal, a center at McBride High School in St. Louis, and offered him a scholarship. St. Louis coach Ed Hickey thought Rosenthal would be his and never forgave Krause for stealing his star. Rosenthal went on to an All-American career at Notre Dame, but he never played for Krause.

In the locker room before the opening game of the 1950-51 season, Krause told his team it would be his last year as basketball coach. It has been rumored for over a year that Krause would step aside to devote himself full time to being athletic director. When he made it official, attention turned first to who might be his successor. Most of the speculation focused on Ray Meyer of DePaul, Johnny Jordan of Loyola and high school coach George Ireland, all Notre Dame graduates. Jordan, a former teammate of Krause's who succeeded Krause as the Irish captain for the 1934–35 season, ultimately got the job.

That would have been a big story if not for the scandal that erupted in college basketball. A Manhattan College player reported that gamblers had bribed him to shave points, the first concrete evidence after years of innuendo. It inspired investigations that implicated thirty-two players from seven schools from 1947 to '50 in point-shaving schemes. Even Kentucky's Alex Groza and Ralph Beard, the best players on the best teams of the era, allegedly were involved.

"Some might call Notre Dame's play that season a scandal as well," Neeley writes. Without their usual penchant for playing to the level of the competition, the Irish had only one upset of note, against St. Louis at the Fieldhouse, which reached its usual fever pitch despite Notre Dame's struggles. That atmosphere may have been the intangible that protected the Irish from a losing season. Krause's last team was a perfect 9-0 at home, but finished a meager 4-11 on the road for a 13-11 mark that left him two wins shy of 100 for his career.

Krause had little time to reflect on his coaching tenure with his administrative duties piling up. Even the university's token of appreciation for his years as basketball coach hinted at the work ahead. Leahy presented Krause with a combination leather briefcase/suitcase at a ceremony before his final home game, as appropriate and useful a gift as he ever received.

CHAPTER

6

Caretaker of the
Rockne Tradition

K**RAUSE INHERITED AN ATHLETIC DEPARTMENT THAT,** in reputation and in practice, embodied the senti- mental ideals long associated with college sports. With Hesburgh under orders to restore a rigid level of authority, stray- ing from the university's self-imposed rules would have been inadvis- able, if not impossible. Krause did not agree with every decision handed down from on-high, but he felt a responsibility to maintain Notre Dame's national good name, to carry on what he considered the "Rockne Tradition."

To Krause, that meant creating an atmosphere where varsity and intramural athletics flourished within a rigorous academic environment, making the lessons of teamwork and sportsmanship an integral part of the curriculum. He believed as deeply in the ancient Greek philosophy of a sound body fostering a sound mind as he did in the Holy Trinity of Father, Son and Holy Spirit. Rockne, dead for two decades but still a vivid specter on campus, made that ideal synonymous with Notre

Dame in both successful intercollegiate competition and vibrant intra-
murals. Krause made his intention to advance that tradition clear in
speeches around the country, like Theodore Roosevelt using his bully
pulpit to inspire the faithful into action:

> My basic philosophy of physical education and athletics is
> best expressed in Latin, once the language of the Church:
> *Mens sana in corpore sano*—'A sound mind in a sound body.'
> The objective we strive for is to develop a well-rounded
> individual, one who is sound in spirit, mind and body. . . .
> A good athletic program is one that will help develop in
> the student those basic characteristics which make him a
> better citizen, help him function as an effective person in a
> democratic society, and teach him to appreciate the rights
> of others . . .
>
> The successful intercollegiate athletic program is based
> on healthy competition against representative opponents
> and can, in my opinion, help develop such desirable charac-
> teristics as: leadership, respect for authority, confidence, loy-
> alty, courage (mental and physical), initiative, strength and
> coordination, teamwork (social awareness), poise, discipline,
> pride in accomplishment . . .
>
> But too often in the search for success in the intercolle-
> giate area, the average student is neglected. This, in my opin-
> ion, must not be and need not be. The importance of a
> vitalized intramural and club sports program, along with a
> good physical education instructional program, is fully rec-
> ognized at the University of Notre Dame.

Krause and the entire Notre Dame hierarchy took that philosophy
seriously, and by all accounts, they pursued their lofty goals with integrity.

In fact, Krause's commitment to those standards exceeded Rockne's. His sense of the legendary coach's ideals came as much from O'Donnell's eulogy and the film *Knute Rockne All-American* as from personal interaction. In Krause's fleeting glimpse of the real Rockne, he encountered a larger-than-life figure. A young, Catholic, aspiring football player, sprung from the stockyards by this charismatic coach, Krause could have felt nothing but gratitude for the opportunity and awe in proximity to such a celebrity.

When the movie starring Pat O'Brien and Ronald Reagan appeared in 1941, it reinforced the romanticized view Krause and many like him carried in their hearts. Rockne's legend and legacy had grown larger in death. *Knute Rockne All-American* solidified his status as Notre Dame's paragon of virtue. That Pat O'Brien's portrayal bore only a passing resemblance to a much more complicated and pragmatic man mattered not at all to Krause. He considered the film a parable that dramatized his beliefs about the value of athletics. It portrayed the "Rockne Tradition" as he understood it. When he became athletic director at Notre Dame, he felt compelled to make that ideal form the foundation of his tenure.

Despite its immaculate reputation, Notre Dame had its share of detractors. Most prominent among them was the National Collegiate Athletic Association. ND and the NCAA clashed over television rights to football games. Suggesting that televised games would reduce attendance, the NCAA sought to pull the plug entirely. Notre Dame argued that its contract with the Dumont network, in place since 1947, had no negative effect on ticket sales, and in fact increased interest in the football program and the university.

Hesburgh negotiated a deal to include extensive programming about campus life in addition to the game itself. "In allowing our games to be televised, we have been able to present sidelight stories on the educational, cultural, and religious aspects of the University of Notre Dame," Krause noted in the midst of the controversy with the NCAA. "And, in itself, this latter [procedure] has become a point of far greater importance to those guiding the destinies of Notre Dame than the mere televising of an athletic contest."

Hesburgh accepted Dumont's $55,000 offer to televise its 1947 season precisely because the other networks, which dangled more money, refused to air what amounted to advertisements for Notre Dame's academic and religious standards. Those spots had an immeasurable impact in advancing the university's mission, burnishing its reputation and filling its coffers far beyond what another network may have offered. That's why Notre Dame officials fought so fiercely to maintain its institutional freedom when the NCAA threatened its autonomy.

Publicly proclaiming television a threat to ticket sales—the financial lifeblood of most athletic departments—the NCAA and many of its members privately disliked Notre Dame's disproportionate financial gains from television because of its national fan base. "The first direct attack on ND's television contract came at the association's 1951 convention," Murray Sperber reports in *Onward to Victory: The Crises That Shaped College Sports*. A resolution ordering a moratorium on individual schools controlling broadcast rights passed overwhelmingly, 161-7.

Hesburgh and Krause became Notre Dame's outspoken opponents of the NCAA decree. It called for only one "Game of the Week" to be televised—with the association choosing the teams—a plan that would cost Notre Dame hundreds of thousands, perhaps millions, in projected broadcast revenues. In 1952, the NCAA decided proceeds from the "Game of the Week" would be distributed among all association members, whether they played a televised game or not, a move Krause decried as akin to Communism.

"In a press report last week, [two proponents of the NCAA policy] said that I was too 'excited' [about the TV revenue-sharing proposal]. My reply to them is, yes, I am excited," Krause declared in October 1952. "Wouldn't you be excited if someone tried to come into your home and steal your furniture? I'll remain excited as long as they try to infringe on the private rights of our institution. I say the plan is illegal, immoral, un-American and socialistic." In the *New York Times,* he jibed, "The NCAA started as an advisory body, then became a regulatory body, and now has become a confiscatory one."

Notre Dame administrators labored over how to respond to the NCAA. They considered challenging the legality of the plan on an anti-trust basis. They even pondered outright defiance in the form of ignoring the NCAA plan and negotiating an independent television contract. Another college football television pioneer, the University of Pennsylvania, had tried that tactic to no avail. The NCAA declared Penn "a member not in good standing" and threatened any team that played the Quakers on television with the same fate. Under pressure, Penn relented.

Offering networks a larger audience than Penn could promise, Notre Dame possessed more power in a potential fight against the NCAA. Membership status in the NCAA might not have mattered to schools that received a check more substantial for one game against Notre Dame than an entire season under a controlled TV plan. That threat convinced the NCAA to abolish its revenue-sharing policy, though it retained control over which games would be televised.

Walking a fine line between independence and arrogance in its national image, Notre Dame felt reluctant to mount a challenge after winning such a concession. Achieving academic and athletic success on its own terms had made the university widely admired, but also a target of jealousy and anti-Catholic bias. Concerned about its public percep-tion in addition to the other swirling issues, and confident that a bad plan would soon fail of its own negative inertia, Notre Dame backed off.

In the process, its contradictory role in modern college athletics took shape. Notre Dame's success and national popularity made it the ultimate insider, a coveted opponent because playing the Irish meant money and notoriety. Yet it often operated apart from the pack, alienating institutions that wanted to replicate its model. At the same time, Notre Dame understood the need to be a part of a national framework to keep itself from being consigned to the fringes of an industry it helped define.

"We have been against the NCAA controlled TV plan for two years," Krause told the *South Bend Tribune* before the 1953 convention, describing their decision on the television issue. "But the NCAA serves a definite purpose in college athletics. There's absolutely no foundation to the story [that ND will resurrect its TV network], even though we strongly oppose controlled TV."

As Sperber explains in *Onward to Victory*, the hypocrisy of the NCAA's position bothered Notre Dame the most. After basketball point-shaving scandals and academic fraud at West Point, the association wanted to appear to be the agent of reform in college sports and to stem the declining attendance in the wake of the disgraces.

Notre Dame stood as a bastion of the disintegrating ideal of the "student-athlete." The academic promotional spots, so integral to the school's independent television broadcasts, disappeared during the NCAA's "Game of the Week." When the university received $50,000 as its share of the revenue in 1952, Krause quipped, "We spent that much money showing the public the advantages of higher education during our TV program two years ago. All this year's program did was try to sell automobiles and sell the NCAA's policy to the public. . . . Instead of films on the academic parts of universities, all you got was some woman named Betty waving at the shelves of a refrigerator . . . and lots of cartoons of dancing light bulbs."

✦ ✦ ✦

Any leverage Notre Dame had in its television dispute came from the success of Frank Leahy, heir to the benefits and burdens of the program Rockne built. From Rockne's death in 1931 until Leahy's arrival a decade later, Notre Dame football had modest success, but never captured the nation's imagination as it had under its charismatic patron saint. Leahy possessed none of Rockne's charm. He even dared to discard Rockne's offense, a sin for which he endured considerable penance. When he started winning—and winning, and winning—with his newfangled T-formation, all was forgiven. Notre Dame again became the national symbol for collegiate athletic success. Leahy ultimately led the Irish to such heights that a *Parade Magazine* profile asked a question that would have been considered sacrilegious not long before: "Greater Than Rockne?"

Thus beatified, Leahy's quest for perfection only increased. Coaching always had a physical effect on him, from vomiting before games to serious stress-related conditions. He brought much of it on himself with a regimen of film study, team meetings, practice, player evaluation, scouting and then, if time permitted, eating and sleeping. Leahy's exhaustive approach to coaching drove him from the game before his time as surely as the plane crash that killed Rockne.

After four consecutive undefeated seasons from 1946 to '49, Leahy's health and Notre Dame's fortunes began to fail. After a mediocre 4-4-1 mark in 1950, the Irish improved to 7-2 each of the next two seasons, but the toll on Leahy became increasingly obvious.

Notre Dame team physician Doctor Nicholas Johns became a confidant of Leahy's. He jokingly called himself the coach's psychiatrist because when they had lunch together three times a week, Leahy reclined on a couch with a sandwich and a glass of milk and talked about anything but football.

Doc Johns developed a close association with the Notre Dame athletic department. He was the family physician to many of the administrators and coaches, and to all of them, he was a friend. Doc Johns and Krause became roommates for road games and served on the board of First United Life Insurance together. They took turns driving to the monthly meetings in Gary, Indiana, and their families often spent summer vacations at the site of the company's annual shareholders retreat.

That intimacy allowed Doc Johns to know more than the medical history of the Notre Dame athletic leadership. He knew what was in their hearts. During their regular lunches and dinners at Leahy's home in Long Beach, near Michigan City, Indiana, Doc Johns shared the private struggles of a very private man. He witnessed the toll of Leahy's relentless intensity up close.

Once the epitome of control on the sidelines, in crisp pinstripe suits and a fedora that made him look more like a chief executive than a coach, Leahy's posture began to droop. A familiar photograph from the early 1950s shows him, hat in hand and head down, looking haggard and drawn, the physical manifestation of the weight on his shoulders.

Much of that weight he placed there himself. As controlling as he was driven, Leahy's diminished role in athletic department policymaking and political battles with Hesburgh must have sapped his spirit as well. Leahy considered his program the model for all to follow, his mission in lockstep with the university's and his means beyond reproach. Any suggestion to the contrary, no matter how amiably made, cut as deeply as any loss.

Leahy also endured the inevitable criticism of fans who had grown accustomed to perfection. Those external influences compounded his own anxiety, quickening a downward spiral that nearly killed him and ultimately forced him to resign at age forty-five. He collapsed at halftime of the 1953 game against Georgia Tech, his condition so grave he received last rites in the locker room from Rev. Edmund P. Joyce, the university's executive vice president. Though he willed one last undefeated season from his 1953 team, his departure appeared inevitable.

"LEAHY QUITS NOTRE DAME" the *Chicago Tribune* proclaimed across the top of its front page on February 1, 1954, when the rumors finally became a reality. Most accounts cited his health, ignoring the institutional politics and external pressures that contributed to his worsening condition. Though it manifested itself physically in his collapse that October afternoon at Notre Dame Stadium, those frustrating factors also took an indelible mental toll. "I have laid down a burden," Leahy said after he announced his resignation.

Hesburgh would say later that Leahy's self-imposed stress and subsequent health problems proved he blew the game out of proportion, a concern the new president had about the university itself and football's rightful place in it. Hesburgh's choice of a successor suggested to many that he planned to diminish the sport's prominence.

Twenty-five-year-old Terry Brennan stepped into Leahy's considerable shadow. With his breakaway runs from the 1940s still fresh in Irish fans' minds, Brennan enjoyed an extended honeymoon and early success as the last of Leahy's players finished their careers. But there were hints about daunting challenges to come. "He's only 25," sports columnist Red Smith wrote when Brennan was hired. "By the time he's 30, he'll be a good deal more than five years older."

Whether through university cutbacks in scholarships and increased academic requirements for athletes, inexperienced and ineffective coaching, or a combination of factors, Brennan's tenure ended badly. He did have some great athletes and glorious moments. Paul Hornung won the 1956 Heisman Trophy as the quarterback for a 2-8 team; and Brennan's Irish beat No. 1 Oklahoma in 1957, ending the longest winning streak in college football history at forty-seven. But Brennan did not have enough great athletes or glorious moments in five years to save his job.

Brennan claims Hesburgh cut scholarships and raised academic standards for athletes to a point that made maintaining Leahy's level of success impossible. "Scholarships were cut somewhat," Francis Wallace writes in *Notre Dame: From Rockne to Parseghian*, "but not to any damaging degree." Another school of thought cites Brennan's hiring of younger assistant coaches rather than retaining Leahy's experienced staff as a factor contributing to his demise.

It's an argument that has gone around and around for a half century. Ultimately, an average record on the field, and some embarrassing incidents off of it, cost Brennan his job in December 1958. He won almost two-thirds of his games, a respectable record though it paled in comparison to Leahy's legacy. In addition, some Irish players caused thousands of dollars in damage to hotel rooms on at least two road trips, most notably after a season-ending loss to USC in 1958. It reinforced the growing impression that Brennan did not have control of the team, another debatable point magnified in comparison to Leahy's legendary demands.

"Even before it happened, there was this feeling that Terry was not a strong enough disciplinarian. That he wasn't big on rules and regulations. That he was too young and liberal for us," former quarterback Don White says in *Talking Irish: The Oral History of Notre Dame Football*. "Personally, I felt it was a bad rap. I think Terry figured: This is Notre Dame. These guys have been hand-picked. They can regulate themselves. But I do think the USC thing hurt him. In fact, I really think it did him in."

In the midst of all this controversy, Krause managed to maintain a neutrality Geneva would have envied. He did not support the decision to give the job to such a young man. Krause respected Brennan as a coach and even predicted a bright future for him at Notre Dame—just not so soon. Brennan's success at Mount Carmel High School in Chicago and a year under Leahy as freshman coach at Notre Dame did not strike Krause as an acceptable resume for an Irish head coach.

Once Brennan came aboard, though, Krause supported him, even befriended him, and never challenged his bosses' decision. "Moose was very helpful any way he could be," Brennan says. "He didn't have a whole lot of authority. Being the athletic director at Notre Dame is a difficult job because you're kind of caught in the middle. We were good friends and he was hurt when I was let go. Unfortunately, he had nothing to say about it."

Krause ultimately had no say in any of the personnel decisions in the athletic department. "None," longtime *South Bend Tribune* sports editor Joe Doyle says. "He had absolutely no say whatsoever." That power resided with Hesburgh, Joyce and the faculty board in control of athletics. "Father Joyce would pick out somebody and tell Moose later," Doc Johns says. "He never complained about it to anybody. Unparalleled loyalty."

Krause's counsel was always valued and he made recommendations when he deemed it necessary, but he trusted Hesburgh and Joyce to make decisions in the best interest of the university. Krause never expressed serious dissent, though after the occasional curious coaching choice he could be heard to mutter under his breath, "The priests at Notre Dame are great people, but they don't know much about football."

No matter how badly the Irish played—and it got worse before it got better after Brennan's unceremonious departure—Krause exuded the unyielding hope that defined Notre Dame's most loyal fan base. What though the odds, as the song said, he believed old Notre Dame would win over all, all evidence to the contrary.

As the public face of the athletic department, Krause had to be upbeat, a condition as natural to him as breathing. With criticism about the football program swirling in the late 1950s and early '60s, Krause's frequent speaking engagements became an important tool for maintaining loyalty, and generosity, among alumni and other fans. Sprinkled liberally with humor, his speeches helped sustain spirited support for Notre Dame, even in times of defeat.

"I know what you all want to hear about, so I'll get right to it," Krause would tease an audience when the football team was in the doldrums. "Once again our fencing team is one of the best in the nation . . ."

He told the story of a priest cloistered in a confessional one Saturday afternoon anxious to know how the Irish were doing. In lieu of penance, the priest sent one boy back to the rectory to listen to a few minutes of the game on the radio and report back. "Bless me, Father," the boy said when he returned. "My last confession was ten minutes ago. I ain't done nothin' and neither has Notre Dame."

Krause defined a successful athletic director as one who, when being chased out of the stadium by a mob of angry fans after a loss, gives the impression he's leading them toward bigger and better things. "Our alumni are extremely fair," he said. "They don't care if we win or lose, as long as we win."

Krause recycled a litany of old jokes with a comic timing even his golfing buddy Bob Hope admired. "They say the trouble with this country is that there is too much ignorance and apathy," Krause would say, pausing for effect. "I don't know what the hell they're talking about and I couldn't care less."

He kept files full of jokes, often of the ethnic, religious or "take my wife . . . please" variety common in that era, adapted to roast any friends in attendance. If his old buddy and former Notre Dame lineman George Connor happened to be in the audience, Krause might inform the crowd that Connor "is very unassuming—and he has every right to be. You know, George would have been Phi Beta Kappa, if it wasn't for his grades."

He even directed some of the barbs at himself. During some of the most difficult times with the football program, Krause said, he found himself sick in the hospital with pneumonia. A note from Father Joyce heartened him. "It said, 'We want to wish you a speedy return to health,'" Krause related. "'The vote was four-to-three by the faculty board.'"

A group of school principals in Columbus, Ohio, once invited him to give a speech about education, Krause said, and he left the podium proud of how well he made his point. "The next day, on my way back to South Bend," he said, "I picked up a Columbus newspaper and the headline read, 'Moose Krause's speech shows need for education.'"

That provided a nice segue into his larger point about the lessons of athletics and their place in a liberal education. "I'm a normal guy, I hate to lose," Krause said, but he placed more importance on the value of competition than the thrill of victory.

Krause's sense of perspective came from a lifetime of personal losses that shaped his outlook on life far more than his victories. Growing up in the Back of the Yards, he had little more than faith to sustain him, the one constant in his life whether he lost a football game or his father. Enduring the Depression and the murder of his father, collecting the remains of fallen soldiers—Krause had seen worse than a 2-8 record.

In late 1952, former basketball player Marty O'Connor, then a law student and an assistant coach to Johnny Jordan, became afflicted with polio. Bed-ridden in a South Bend hospital for four months, he became acquainted with Krause on a deeper level than he ever had when he played for him. Stripped down to his underwear and swathed in itchy, wool blankets, O'Connor lay in bed with little to occupy him but self-pity. Krause boosted his spirits with regular visits. He cheered up O'Connor even as he choked up. "This giant of a man would pull his chair right up to my bed," O'Connor says. "There would be tears in that giant of a man's eyes. He could cry, and still laugh."

Krause asked his old friend Abe Saperstein of the Harlem Globetrotters if he would be willing to play a benefit game at Notre Dame to help offset O'Connor's medical bills. Saperstein agreed immediately, telling Krause for the first time that he had overheard his angry response years earlier to the promoter who wanted to cheat the Globetrotters out of their share of the gate receipts. O'Connor's benefit became the first of many exhibitions the Globetrotters staged at Notre Dame. Though he spent the rest of his life in a wheelchair, O'Connor went on to a successful law career.

Two years later, another tragedy struck the Notre Dame family that affected Krause even more deeply. His busy schedule as athletic director forced him to cancel a planned ice-fishing trip to Canada with his old friend Fred Miller just before Christmas, 1954. Miller's eldest son, Fred Jr., a Notre Dame student at the time, hustled home to Milwaukee when his semester ended, just in time to catch the brewing company's private plane for the trip up to the family cabin.

As the twin-engine Lockheed Ventura leveled off after departure on a snowy night from Milwaukee's Mitchell Field, witnesses reported a burst of flame and the aircraft suddenly lurching toward the ground. Fred Jr. and the two pilots died at the scene, while the elder Miller survived for several hours after being thrown from the wreckage and suffering burns over 50 percent of his body. He died later that night, leaving the Milwaukee and Notre Dame communities he enriched with so much more than his money mourning their loss.

Miller came to Notre Dame in the mid 1920s as an heir to millions. Krause followed a few years later with little more than the scent of the stockyards in his meager wardrobe. They both achieved athletic stardom and professional success, yet possessed an endearing ability to erase the social divisions their stature could have created. "I remember

Dad always had a very prominent picture of Fred Miller. That was his best buddy," Krause's youngest son, Phil, says. "They just had the same disposition."

Arch Ward, the longtime sports editor and columnist at the *Chicago Tribune*, attended a gathering with his son at Krause's home on the eve of the final home football game of the 1954 season. After meeting Miller for the first time at the party, Ward's son remarked to his father, "Gee, you never would think Fred was a multimillionaire, would you?" Red Smith, whose years at Notre Dame overlapped with Miller's, put it this way: "He was rough and reliable and rich, but only the first two attributes were noticeable."

Fred Miller embodied Rudyard Kipling's "If," a poem Krause tried to live by.

> If you can talk with crowds and keep your virtue
> Or walk with kings—nor lose the common touch . . .
> If neither foes nor loving friends can hurt you
> If all men count with you but none too much . . .
> Yours is the earth and everything that's in it
> And—which is more—you'll be a man my son!

Krause sobbed when he heard the news of Miller's death, out of sadness for his friend, of course, but no doubt also out of shock because he had planned to be aboard that plane until just days earlier. After all the turmoil the Krause family had endured, from their frequent moves to Ed's hectic coaching and playing schedules to the tense uncertainty of the war, they finally had settled into a stable lifestyle. With a comfortable new home on leafy Peashway Street near the campus, a healthy family and a rewarding job without the stress of coaching, Krause felt a sense of serenity. Miller's death reminded him of the fragility of it all.

Always sensitive to the fact that his job took him away from home more than he would have liked, Krause made a point to be especially attentive and involved whenever he spent time with his children. He seemed impossibly big to them then, yet warm and comfortable too. Mary would climb on his lap and he would stroke her blond hair, asking about school and friends, appearing as interested in dolls and multiplication tables as the fullback trap. "I always felt like I had his undivided attention," Mary says.

With his big body splayed on the living room floor, he helped Eddie assemble a Lionel train set and watched it run around and around, through a tunnel and out the other side. He also taught his sons the nuances of blocking and shooting a basketball. Though neither Eddie nor Phil possessed their father's talent, he insisted they participate, much as his parents had once demanded music lessons.

In the summertime, Krause converted an old military raft into a makeshift backyard "pool." When he floated in it, little room remained for the kids. So he would hop out and splash them and dunk them. Their high-pitched laughter became the soundtrack of lazy summer weekends. Krause's baritone and the boom-boom-boom of his feet hitting the ground as he chased them around the yard provided the beat.

All this horseplay happened only after homework and chores had been completed. Elise saw to that. "She was a regimented German," Phil says. Krause called her the "Little General." When her sister's family visited in the summer, Elise would give all the children jobs to complete before they could go out and play. "No project was too small," her niece Dorothy Sippel says. "She was great on telling everyone what to do."

Eddie and Mary submitted to Elise's authority at an early age. Phil resisted. Family photos from the mid-1950s show Eddie and Mary dressed neatly with angelic smiles. Phil's tousled hair, cocked head and crooked ties reflect the mischievous glint in his eyes. As he grew up, his penchant for shunning chores and homework became chronic and his parents decided he needed the discipline of boarding school. Elise enrolled Phil at the rigorous Campion Prep School in Prairie du Chein, Wisconsin. Known for its strict disciplinary codes, which set Phil on a path that ultimately led him to Notre Dame, Krause sold him on the idea from an athletic angle. "He said, 'It has every sport except archery,'" Phil says. "He didn't tell me about the discipline part, but he did a helluva sales job."

Krause often found himself selling Elise on the benefits of family vacation destinations. When he sought solace from his responsibilities at Notre Dame and elsewhere, Krause would use his extensive connections to plan a private family getaway. Elise did not always like Krause's ideas, but the results usually pleased her.

When he informed her the president of the Cannon Towel Company invited them to use his cabin on the Pierre-Marquette River in Michigan, Elise reluctantly agreed. Not an aficionado of roughing it, the idea of "a little cabin in the woods," as Krause described it, did not appeal to her. They packed sleeping bags and sandwiches and other assorted supplies for a weekend away from civilization. "We get up there and it's just a huge log mansion that rambled forever," Phil says. "He had a tackle house bigger than most people's homes."

A private chef prepared their meals. Cannon owned seven miles of riverfront, where Krause could spend relaxing early mornings catching trout for the chef to cook. Krause always returned proud of his impressive catch. "We'd kid him, 'You didn't catch that. There's no way you caught all that,'" Mary says. One morning the kids woke up early and spotted Krause not on one of the many piers on Cannon's property jutting into the river, but in a prestocked trout pond. Caught like one of Cannon's captive fish, an embarrassed Krause said, "They weren't biting today on the river, so I decided to go in here."

Another morning, Mary and Eddie decided to make blueberry pancakes for breakfast. As they were preparing to pour the batter on the griddle, Mary asked Eddie if he had added the sugar. He could not remember, so Mary suggested he add two cups. As it turned out, Eddie had included the sugar in the first place and the recipe called for only two tablespoons, not two cups. "We put in four cups of sugar," Mary says. They peeled the pancakes off the griddle, paper thin and sweeter than a pastry, and placed them on a plate for Krause.

"What's this?" he said.

"It's blueberry pancakes," Mary said.

"Blueberry what? You're sure it's not candy?"

They assured him he had blueberry pancakes in front of him and he grudgingly reached for the syrup when Elise sat down to breakfast and surveyed his plate.

"What are you eating, Ed?" she said.

"Well, Mother, I think I'm eating candy," Krause said, "but the kids say it's blueberry pancakes."

Krause ate much better when he spent a weekend on a six-hundred-foot Inland Steel ore carrier. A high-ranking friend at the company invited Krause and his family for a ride. "I'm not going on that tramp steamer," Elise said. Krause weakened her resistance with promises of opulence that sounded hollow, especially when they arrived at the loading dock with the mill's smokestacks belching in the background. Soot covered the boat as they boarded. "Oh boy, this doesn't look good," Elise said. When they were led to the captain's quarters below deck, her outlook changed. "There were assorted bedrooms. Very plush. Just gorgeous," Phil says. "The meals were exquisite. Dad loved it because he could relax, he didn't have to do anything. They waited on you hand and foot. Mother shut up right away."

✦ ✦ ✦

In a tacit acknowledgment of their mistake in hiring Terry Brennan, Notre Dame administrators tried the opposite approach in naming his successor as football coach. They chose experience over potential, an authoritarian presence over a laissez-faire leader. Yet in a sense, they hired the same man. Though their personalities and approach to the game varied, both Brennan and Joe Kuharich suffered from the same failure to communicate their vision to their players. To be successful, college coaches need to teach, to motivate and to build an atmosphere of confidence.

Krause often wandered out to the practice field on autumn afternoons, usually just to watch for his own interest, as any football fan with such unfettered access would have. Yet he had an eye attuned to a coach's technique and an ear attuned to a team's attitude. He absorbed more on a stroll along the sidelines at practice than his demeanor ever revealed. When Irish fortunes faltered, he understood why, the shortcomings in tactics and talent evident from his visits to the practice field.

"In '56 when they were losing [under Brennan], he was out there at practice and being very observant. . . . By '62 he was out there again, looking and knowing he was going to make a recommendation to the athletic board [to fire Kuharich]," Joe Doyle says. "Had Kuharich not left, Moose would have recommended that they not rehire him, because he could not see eye-to-eye with Kuharich. He knew he was a bad coach."

Krause experienced many of the disappointing days of the Kuharich era over and over again, like a recurring bad dream. As a color analyst on Notre Dame football broadcasts with "Mr. Sports himself, Harry Wismer," Krause relived every game in a recording studio. After the live film had been edited for the Sunday morning replay, a laconic Krause and an excitable Wismer read their commentary from a script prepared for them in advance. In his best broadcasters' inflection, Krause conveyed information about the weather, players' size and hometowns, and basic Xs and Os.

This elaborate process began in 1959, Kuharich's first season, requiring technical and logistical planning akin to the space program, as

South Bend Tribune television editor Jim McNeile described. "Putting Notre Dame football into millions of living rooms hours after the Saturday afternoon games," McNeile wrote, "seems every bit as intricate as firing a payload to the moon."

It required editing a videotape of the game down to an hour and preparing a script for Wismer and Krause, who hustled to the nearest studio to record their comments all within hours after the game. When Notre Dame played the University of California at Berkeley in 1959, they had to fly to Los Angeles for the taping, arriving at the CBS Studios with about five minutes to spare.

A ravenous national appetite for Notre Dame football inspired the plan—indeed, the Irish replays became as much a Sunday morning ritual as Mass for many fans across the country. They could not have liked what they saw under Kuharich. Krause certainly did not, though on the air he praised Notre Dame's "very fine coaching staff."

Kuharich came from the Washington Redskins to coach at his alma mater, and his professional approach did not translate. He never developed a rapport with the players, never earned their respect. By the end of Kuharich's tenure in 1962, quarterback Daryle Lamonica simply disregarded some of his play calls. Kuharich resigned in the spring of 1963 with a 17-23 record—the only Notre Dame coach ever to have a losing record. Notre Dame officials did not initiate his departure, but they welcomed the news that Kuharich would become the NFL's supervisor of officials.

Freshman coach Hugh Devore, who had been an interim coach during World War II, stepped in again to help Notre Dame out of a jam. Because Kuharich left in the spring, the timing made it impossible to consider outside candidates. One of Notre Dame's most loyal sons, Devore was a popular choice among players and fans alike. Everyone hoped he would have enough success to make this temporary arrangement permanent. From the start, it was clear it would not last as Notre Dame limped to another miserable 2-7 season.

This persistent football malaise mystified and frustrated fans. De-emphasis became a buzzword bandied about at banquets and cocktail parties. Prevailing wisdom suggested Notre Dame administrators wanted football to fail, insisting on academic standards so strict and scholarship numbers so limited it put the Irish at a competitive disadvantage.

Nobody in power ever considered deliberately deemphasizing football. They pursued excellence in all endeavors, football included. Hesburgh and Joyce may have been naive in their belief that the Irish could win on lofty ideals alone, but they wanted both victory and vindi-cation for their approach. It took ten frustrating seasons under Brennan and Kuharich—seasons of embarrassing disarray, if not deemphasis—to find a coach who could fulfill that vision.

✦ ✦ ✦

They found him in Evanston, Illinois, though he did not have the Notre Dame pedigree that had previously been a prerequisite. He did, how-ever, have a history of success as a head coach at Miami of Ohio and Northwestern, unassailable integrity and the intensity necessary to restore Notre Dame's football reputation. So began the courtship of an Armenian Protestant named Ara Parseghian.

Innocent flirting had been going on for a few years. Parseghian vis-ited South Bend to speak at a banquet in the late 1950s, playing golf with Krause and striking up a friendship that, at first, would yield only a foot-ball series between Notre Dame and Northwestern. When Parseghian's Wildcats made defeating the Irish an annual ritual, Notre Dame admin-istrators sensed that he possessed intangible leadership qualities their own recent coaches had not. Parseghian's feelings for Notre Dame grew after each victory over the Irish, when Hesburgh, Joyce and Krause vis-ited the Northwestern locker room to offer congratulations. "I'd never experienced this before at any Big Ten school, or any school I had ever coached at," Parseghian says. "I thought that was such a classy act, to have the president, the executive vice president and the athletic director come to your locker room and congratulate the team and staff; I was so impressed with that because it never happened before."

Their mutual admiration firmly established, the impending consummation of the relationship between Parseghian and Notre Dame became an open secret by December 1963. The *South Bend Tribune* published a story about the hiring of the new coach and the press was summoned to the Morris Inn on campus for the official announcement.

As he drove up Notre Dame Avenue on the day of his planned public introduction, Parseghian felt a chill run up his spine. For the first time, he sensed the magnitude of the job. Combined with Notre Dame's struggling football program and the break from tradition his hiring would represent, Parseghian needed more time to ponder his decision. Notre Dame's Catholic tradition and its recent football failures troubled him. He read a statement saying the news of his hiring had been premature and abruptly left the press conference.

Krause, who would become a big brother figure and loyal confidant of Parseghian's for the next eleven years, helped assuage his concerns. "Notre Dame hadn't had a winning season in five years, and the suggestion was that Father Hesburgh had made this an academic institution, which is fine, but it was such an academic institution now that . . . football was diminished, in scholarship numbers and so forth. I heard the rumors, I did not know that for a fact," Parshegian says. "Those are some of the things I remember discussing with Moose, asking him specifically, 'What about the situation here? Is there a specific effort to downgrade and downplay athletics and specifically football, because this is to be the Yale of the Midwest?'"

Dismissing that as an unfounded rumor, Krause assured Parseghian he belonged at Notre Dame and offered a candid assessment of the football program that convinced him to accept the job. "Ara, I think you're going to find better talent here than you realize," Krause said. "Yes, we haven't won for a number of reasons, but talent is not necessarily one of them."

✦ ✦ ✦

Traveling for speaking engagements, meetings and football games was an inevitable part of being Notre Dame's athletic director. Never had Krause traversed the country as tirelessly as he did in the mid-1960s, raising money for a new campus athletic facility. "He and I operated by phone," his secretary Eleanor VanDerHagen says. "He would only come home rarely and was gone again because he went to all parts of the country to stimulate the alumni." He visited 175 cities, raising most of the $8.6 million needed to construct the Athletic and Convocation Center, the first major building project on campus involving varsity athletics since the football stadium in 1930.

Krause also became involved in so many civic and religious projects that, in football parlance, he could have been flagged for piling on. Twice he flew to Europe to speak at Catholic retreats for soldiers. He chaired the South Bend Parks and Recreation Commission from its inception in 1965 until his death and served on several corporate boards.

Krause's work with the Parks and Recreation Commission, a program funded by both the school corporation and the city government, could have been limited to his name on the letterhead. Instead, he used his position to amplify his ideas about the importance of athletic participation in the community beyond Notre Dame. When budget cuts threatened to trim the department's services, Krause attended school board and city council meetings long into the night to lobby for the cause. "He would invariably appear before the council or the school board," recreation commission president Bob Goodrich says, "and just his being there persuaded them that this was important.

"We took advantage of him, I know," Goodrich adds, "asking him to speak at state conventions and other programs. I don't think he ever said no."

Often Krause didn't even have to be asked for his support. When racial unrest in South Bend festered into violent outbursts in the late 1960s, he conceived a program called "Reach Up" to help mend the wounds. For two summers, Notre Dame assistant basketball coaches took the Irish team, featuring players like Austin Carr, to different parks around town to participate in pick-up games against South Bend residents. A Notre Dame exhibition game during the basketball season between the two summers funded the program. As many as three thousand people turned out to watch some of the games, which "really helped draw the community back together," Goodrich says. "Anything written about it, you won't even see Moose's name mentioned, but he really set it up."

Krause also set up Notre Dame's imposing football schedules, which often found the Irish playing the nation's best teams and most prominent programs week after week. As an independent team with national interest, Notre Dame played from coast to coast, filling spots when opponents did not have a conference game and giving its far-flung alumni a glimpse of the team.

Krause considered it a badge of honor to have a difficult schedule. Notre Dame forged its reputation under Rockne by challenging and defeating the best teams in the nation. To stray from that would have been to deny the Irish football heritage, something Krause refused to do. He relished the competition, even if it meant explaining a few losses to the alumni in the offseason.

"We teased Dad," Eddie Krause says, "about his possessing Cicero's oratorical skills, Constantine's military prowess, and the underdog stamina of the persecuted Christians."

Krause maintained his rigorous routine because Elise kept their home life in such meticulous order he never had to give it a thought. She did everything from making the beds to paying the bills, from cooking meals to correcting homework, from dishes to discipline.

Every Sunday, to acknowledge her hard work, Krause gave Elise "the day off." Cooking scrambled eggs and corned beef hash for breakfast or barbecued ribs for dinner, he loved to show off his prowess in the kitchen. He tried to follow his mother's recipe for baking bread, but it never turned out as well as Grandma Krause's. On special occasions, he prepared pheasant with pork stuffing and a broccoli soufflé. Krause hated traditional bread stuffing—"Why would you want to put bread in a turkey?" he often wondered—so he created a meat substitute that remains a family Thanksgiving staple. "It was like stuffing a meatloaf into the turkey," Mary says, laughing. "But it was delicious. I still do that."

All the Krause children have warm memories of their father, cigar in his mouth and spatula in his hand, standing over a hot stove on the pretense of giving Elise a break. He loved to cook and usually left extra work for Elise in his wake. "My mom would get mad at him because the kitchen would be destroyed," Mary says. "She'd say, 'It'll take me all day Monday to clean up what you did on Sunday.'" Krause would just chuckle and offer his calming refrain, "Now, Mother," and roll up his sleeves to do the dishes.

Though Elise's strength seemed evident to everyone as soon as they met her, Krause maintained a protective instinct that amused their friends. When she traveled to Rome in 1964 to visit their son Eddie, who was studying to be a priest, Krause wrote a letter to his Notre Dame classmate Vince McAloon. He lived in Rome, teaching English, ethics and public speaking at Notre Dame International, an American prep school. A concerned Krause, at great length, asked McAloon to watch over Elise.

"I'll never forget the letter because it was endless, single-spaced," McAloon says. "He was so worried over the fact that his wife was going over there to visit Eddie. He sounded like a big baby. He said, 'She's never been away before and you must look after her.' When she arrived, she was a storm. She was a leader. She took over, against the background of Moose's trembling letter. She plops down on the floor of the lounge, opens a big map and starts planning her conquest of Rome. I always thought back to Moose's letter. 'Help my poor wife.'"

✦ ✦ ✦

Parseghian likewise asserted immediate control over the Notre Dame football program. Just as Elise Krause commanded situations with the electric power of her personality, Parseghian turned routine meetings into revivals. He made football players believe in him and each other and the inspirational power of the Notre Dame spirit.

"This team had a fire that blazed to the sky in the past. Perhaps the flame has burned low of late, but it's not out," Parseghian tells players he inherited from the Kuharich era in Tom Pagna's *Era of Ara*. "You guys could possibly be the first Notre Dame class ever to graduate without having a winning year. You don't want that and neither do I. Within this room we have the makings of a great football team. We'll have to work. It's not going to be easy. But if you want it badly enough we can do it." Nobody wanted it more than Parseghian himself, the dark intensity of his eyes providing a window into his competitive soul. He burned to win. And he fanned that smoldering fire within the Irish players.

Parseghian constructed a championship contender in 1964 with the talent inherited from Devore's 2-7 team. Moving several players to positions that better suited their skills and showing confidence in a shy, obscure quarterback named John Huarte, he changed the identity of the Irish as dramatically as he changed their appearance. Discarding stripes on the jerseys and shamrocks on the helmets, Parseghian restored unornamented blue and gold and the weekly expectation of victory.

Parseghian never expected the frenzy that followed the Notre Dame traveling party, a constant presence—some might say distraction—no matter how well the Irish were playing. Most of them wanted to have a drink with Moose or hear him tell their favorite story again or just shake his oversized paw for good luck.

"You couldn't go anywhere, I swear. My first year I was amazed," Parseghian says. "On all our road trips, you walked in the hotel lobby and there were tons of people running up to Moose. He had friends everywhere. I've never seen a guy, never been around anybody that had as many friends as Moose Krause did. You could just count on it, as soon as he walked into that lobby—wham!—they were all over the place."

Notre Dame's 1964 renaissance only increased the size of the crowds that followed the Irish everywhere they went. They traveled to Los Angeles with a 9-0 record and only traditional rival USC standing between them and a national title. With a 17-0 halftime lead, hearts started beating a little faster and palms felt a little clammy among the Irish traveling party. Nobody felt the emotion of the moment more than Krause, who considered the Armenian-Protestant with the degree from Miami of Ohio the best example of a "Notre Dame man" he had encountered since the Leahy era.

Krause knew Parseghian did not need a championship for validation after all he had accomplished in less than a year since accepting the job. But he felt the coach deserved it for just that reason. Anything less feels empty at Notre Dame and Parseghian's remarkable resuscitation of the program would not hold its rightful place in history without the No. 1 ranking bestowed upon it. So it hurt Krause as deeply as Parseghian when it all slipped away in the second half against USC, a 17-0 lead becoming a 20-17 loss in a blur.

Still, the Irish finished third in the nation and John Huarte, whose voice could barely be heard in the huddle as a third-string quarterback a year earlier, won the Heisman Trophy. Parseghian had restored Notre

Dame's football tradition. After the initial sting of the loss subsided, that satisfied Krause even as Parseghian felt more driven to accomplish what had been so tantalizingly close in 1964.

Parseghian took some solace in the players' response on the way home from Los Angeles. "During the flight some of the seniors came to him and thanked him for the year," Tom Pagna writes in *Notre Dame's Era of Ara*. "They had heard the same 'We're going to win' phrases from other coaches in the past. But the difference was that Ara made them see *how* they could win because of all the elements that went into it—organization, strategy, conditioning, and, mostly, morale. He had brought them farther than any of them imagined possible, from 2-7 to third in the nation in just one year."

Like Leahy a generation earlier, Parseghian's success increased expectations among fans. Notre Dame lost two games and tied one in his second season, a disappointment after the success of his first year.

Even the route to a national championship in 1966 had its disorienting detours, including one that nearly knocked Notre Dame off course in perhaps its biggest game since the famous 0-0 tie against Army twenty years earlier. Parseghian endured considerable criticism after a 10-10 tie against Michigan State at East Lansing for his conservative play calling late in the game.

A week later Notre Dame defeated USC 51-0 in Los Angeles to solidify the No. 1 ranking that slipped away at the Coliseum two years earlier. That won everybody over to Ara's side.

"I remember a guy by the name of Hughie Mulligan in Chicago," Krause said. "He had seen Notre Dame play for many, many years. When we hired Ara, he called and said, 'Moose, I take exception to the fact that you hired a Presbyterian, a Protestant, to be coach at Notre Dame. Why couldn't you hire a fighting Irishman, a Catholic, to be the head of our team?'"

"This man is a good man, Hughie, a fine gentleman, an inspiring figure," Krause said. "He's doing a great job."

He could not persuade Mulligan, who pledged never to watch Notre Dame play again. After a 25-2-2 record and a national championship in three seasons under Parseghian, the phone rang again in Krause's office.

"That Protestant's not doing too bad," Mulligan said.

"Hughie, I'm glad you called," Krause said. "One thing I forgot to tell you is that Rockne was a Protestant when he came to Notre Dame and after a few years we converted him."

"Well, maybe someday we'll convert Ara."

"Look Hughie, the way Ara's going, he's liable to convert all of us."

Krause and his family traveled to Rome just before Christmas, 1966, for Edward Jr.'s ordination as a Holy Cross priest, one of their most meaningful journeys together. Even Krause's old Marine Corps chaplain Father Gannon, a frequent golfing buddy and guest for football games, made the trip. He had promised years earlier to attend Ed's ordination, assuming it would be at Notre Dame. Despite the distance, he kept his promise.

Still basking in the satisfaction of the first national championship since the Leahy era, Krause nearly burst with pride as his son prepared to fulfill an ambition he once had for himself. Every cigar felt like a celebration. Krause's classmate Vince McAloon, who helped organize their trip, operated a hospitality center in Rome for Notre Dame alumni and taught the six-piece Neopolitan band at the restaurant Scoglio di Frisio to play the Victory March. In the shadow of the Vatican, the Krause family felt as close to home as they did to God.

His Excellency Bishop Canestri of the Rome Vicarate ordained Rev. Edward Krause, CSC on December 17, 1966, a moment as moving to Krause as any in his life. In his son, Krause saw the faded image of himself as a priest vividly renewed.

After a private audience with Pope Paul VI and the other newly ordained priests and their families, the Krauses began a pilgrimage to Pompeii and Herculaneum, Paestum and Monte Casino, Assisi and Florence. Krause made a special point to stop at the beaches of Anzio to pray for fallen soldiers. With 250,000 others, they celebrated Christmas in St. Peter's Square before visiting the Catacombs and the Circus Maximus. Ever the athletic director, Krause marveled at its "seating capacity," estimated at about 300,000. He alluded often to Peter as the "Rock" on which the Catholic Church was founded, and Rockne as the "Rock" on which Notre Dame's athletic traditions were built, his two religions forever intertwined.

Both had given him moments of joy in recent weeks. Parseghian had restored the football glory of Rockne and Leahy, success Krause felt a responsibility to perpetuate as athletic director. Now his son had achieved a personal triumph he cheered more than any championship. Krause felt at peace with the world.

Until tragedy struck with the sudden, debilitating force of a blizzard.

A Veritable Crucifixion

SNOWY WEATHER ON THE INDIANA TOLL ROAD delayed Krause's return from a First United Life Insurance board meeting in Gary on January 21, 1967. He called Elise to say he and Doc Johns would be late. They had planned to attend a cocktail party before hosting a dinner that evening for a group of international students. Krause suggested she call a neighbor for a ride.

"No, that's okay," Elise said. "I'll just call a cab."

Two weeks removed from their Roman holiday, Ed and Elise had resumed the familiar, rapid rhythm of their lives. While Ed ran from meetings to games to speaking engagements, Elise ran their social calendar with her usual regimented authority. Though she would be serving dinner to a dozen students in a few hours, she never considered skipping the university cocktail party, one of countless similar gatherings she had attended over the years. Elise would represent her husband, making apologies for his absence, fulfilling what they considered an obligation to be active members of the extended Notre Dame community.

Thumbing through the phone book, Elise called Indiana Cab because the owner had been a friend of the family for years. As the taxi rolled down Peashway Street to Notre Dame Avenue, then south to Corby Boulevard and east toward her destination, she gazed out the window at dirty plowed snow on the curbs and barren trees, the usual winter scenery. A thick, dark blanket of clouds foreshadowed an approaching storm, probably the snow already blowing east off of Lake Michigan delaying Krause's drive from Gary.

Sitting in the driver's seat with his cigar nearly suffocating Doc Johns, Krause toddled along the slick Toll Road at about 40 miles per hour. He pushed it up to about 50 when he noticed a state police car trailing them. But the officer intended only to escort them. He bore bad news that would have made Krause speed home. If they had made an extended stop, he would have told them, but instead he just followed to assure they reached Exit 77 at South Bend as quickly and safely as possible.

A car had run a stop sign at Oak Ridge and Corby, crashing into Elise's cab and spinning it into a telephone pole. Thrown from side to side in the back seat, she suffered massive head injuries and many broken bones. By the time Krause heard the news from Doc Johns' wife, Doris, Elise was in intensive care at St. Joseph's Hospital. He drove there in a daze through the thick flakes of lake effect snow that had followed him all the way home.

✦ ✦ ✦

Doctors did not expect Elise to live through the night. "She would have been killed if she had not had her fur coat on," Doc Johns says. "She had liver damage, brain damage, broken bones every place." Mary, home from Barat College for her winter break, met Krause at the hospital. Elise's sister, Dorothy Feeney, drove through the storm from Chicago, bringing Phil from Campion Prep School. They kept a tense vigil at the hospital, the nauseating and heart-rending sight of Elise illustrating the doctors' bleak prognosis. "When we got into that hospital room, I got sick to my stomach," Feeney says. "Her head was split right open."

As Elise lay unconscious, with oxygen tubes inflating her punctured lungs and life support systems maintaining her body's precarious connection to her brain, Krause refused to accept what everyone else considered inevitable. "She's not going to die," became his mantra. He stroked her face and tapped her feet, talking to her as if they were reminiscing across the dinner table.

She did not stir. "My mother was not responding to anything," Mary says. "We'd go and we'd talk and talk and talk, three times a day, nothing." Yet Krause felt an obligation to make the three fifteen-minute visits the hospital allowed every day, no matter the circumstances. As the snow piled up on the streets one evening, it made driving impossible, so he told Mary to put on her skis.

"I can't miss it. I just can't do it," he said. "My sweetheart knows when I'm there."

Together they skied down Hill Street toward the hospital, sloshing through the doors, wet and weighed down with equipment, much to the shock of the staff who wondered how anyone could have traveled on a night like that. They ignored the fifteen-minute limit that night.

Elise's condition slowly stabilized, though she remained confined to her bed in intensive care, unable to eat, drifting in and out of a hazy consciousness. While doctors could not precisely determine the extent of damage to her brain, her physical deterioration happened before everyone's eyes. Her weight plummeted from 145 to 98 pounds in three months, when the hospital finally moved her to a private room.

Free from the tubes that had provided her only nourishment for months, Elise still did not have the strength to stand. Riddled with bedsores in addition to the residual pain of broken bones and bruises, she had been reduced to a brittle skeleton. Yet that visible evidence did not begin to reveal the depth of the damage done. As she became more alert, a new, volatile personality emerged, as if a different soul inhabited her shell of a body.

She still recognized her family. Krause kept a picture of himself and the pope beside Elise's hospital bed, asking her to identify them. "Which one do you like best?" he teased, and she would point a crooked finger at his photo. When the mood struck her, though, she would lash out. Elise's cutting remarks could be directed at anyone, her husband included. Krause would pat her arm and say, "Now, Mother," calming her until the next verbal spasm.

At the slightest discomfort, Elise would repeatedly push the button to summon the nurse, who she called the operator. "Get the operator in here!" she would bellow. "Operator! Operator!" Even after she was able to eat, she refused food so adamantly she had to be force-fed. "I can remember trying to shove food down her throat and my dad doing the same thing," Mary says.

Whatever physical strength those forced morsels provided, nothing could restore her personality. Those closest to Elise resigned themselves to the idea that, though her life no longer appeared to be in danger, they had lost her. She communicated mostly through blurted commands and insults, the damage to the emotional bank of her brain more debilitating than any broken bone.

Krause refused to believe it would be permanent. "He always thought my mom would bounce back," Mary says. "I'd say, 'Dad, she's not going to be normal. They've told us that.'" He authorized several surgical procedures, hoping the damage could be undone. Doctors even inserted a shunt to relieve pressure from fluid building up on Elise's brain. Nothing worked.

All the strain began to take a destructive emotional toll on Krause. Adding to his anguish, his mother died while Elise was in the hospital, leaving him without the comfort and companionship of the two strongest women in his life. Krause's drinking became chronic. He started bringing a bottle of scotch to Elise's hospital room as a personal prescription for his pain.

As the months wore on it became clear nothing could ease Elise's suffering. Doctors insisted she be transferred to an extended care facility. No amount of alcohol diminished Krause's stubborn belief that his wife would be well again one day. He told them he would take Elise home.

"We're not equipped," Mary said.

He dismissed her concerns. "I'm going to take her home."

Mary had decided soon after the accident not to return to Barat College, enrolling at Saint Mary's in South Bend to be close to home where she could help with her mother's care. Elise's sister Dorothy Feeney and their Aunt Rose also made extended visits.

Damaged tendons in her hand and broken bones in her arm made it impossible for Elise to bathe and feed herself. She still could not walk, so Krause carried her up and down the stairs each day. When she started mustering a few steps before her balance wavered, he would follow close behind, poised to catch her like a toddler.

Elise never made any strides mentally. She responded to stimuli, her approval or disapproval readily apparent, but her reactions were instinctive not intellectual. Some people—usually women, though often Krause himself—endured her rage over things as trivial as the style of a dress or the sound of ice in her glass. "Ed never once raised his voice to her," Dorothy says. "I don't know how he did it. I would have to go home to recuperate, she was such a tyrant."

No matter how debilitated she became, she could relate memories from her life in vivid detail; she beamed at any mention of her son the priest, who could do no wrong in her mind as long as he wore that collar; and she never forgot the Hail Mary or the Our Father. Yet Elise never again possessed a rational understanding of the world around her.

She lived entirely inside her damaged mind with no filter between her emotions and her actions.

For all the support family and friends provided in caring for Elise, Krause carried the brunt of the emotional burden himself. He had suffered the greatest loss. The multilayered relationship of their strong marriage, the love and trust and intimacy and comfort they had shared for twenty-nine years, ended in an instant. "She was never a companion again after the accident," Mary's husband, Sandy Carrigan, says. "She could relate incidents from the past like they were yesterday, she could say all her prayers, but she couldn't sit down and have a conversation. Their relationship stopped in terms of growth or friendship or any of those things."

Despite that, their relationship endured. Even as he drifted deeper into an alcoholic daze, Krause's commitment to Elise grew stronger as his heart and his willpower weakened.

There were good times in the midst of the suffering. When Father Ed offered his first Mass in the summer of 1967, Elise summoned the strength to attend, the first time she had been out since the accident. It was a physical strain, but she beamed as her son took his place on the altar in the vestments she had revered all her life.

Two years later, Mary and Sandy Carrigan were married in an emotional ceremony at St. Joseph's Church in South Bend. Mary fell in love with Sandy, she says, "because he reminded me of my father." The happy couple surprised Father Ed with the news of their engagement through the screen in a confessional. "People waiting in line must have been perplexed," Father Ed says, "as we rushed out of the confessional and into the church vestibule so I could see the wedding ring and give them a hug."

Father Ed performed the ceremony, "one of the happiest and most beautiful occasions, filled with real family love," Marie Virgil, a member of the choir that performed at the Mass, wrote in a letter to Elise. As

Mary stepped off the altar with Sandy, she leaned over and kissed her mother, who glowed as much as the bride herself.

On the surface, it appeared the Krauses had restored a semblance of normalcy to their lives. Elise started attending social events again and appeared physically well, though the residual effects of badly broken bones made eating and drinking difficult. Her outbursts provided evidence of the damage within. Krause never expressed embarrassment or anger toward her, no matter how outrageous her comments. A woman once walked by in a low-cut dress and Elise screamed, "You're boobs are showing!" Another time, an old friend hugged her and she shrieked, "Get away from me! You're fat!" Krause just leaned over to her as he always did and whispered, "Now, Mother."

Everyone from Hesburgh to Parseghian to his own family canonized Krause for the restraint and respect he exuded long after the accident had robbed Elise of those qualities. Eleanor VanDerHagen remembers Krause walking into the office with cuts and bruises on his arms. "She would attack him with anything—fireplace equipment, brooms, you name it," VanDerHagen says. "He never complained. He would come in and go, 'Look El, what Mother did to me today.'"

"I call him Saint Edward, because he was truly a saint," Parseghian says. "The way he treated his wife after this accident, it is a great example of a human being, and if every person had that kind of compassion and understanding and respect for his spouse, this would be a helluva lot better world."

"Just absolutely the Rock of Gibraltar, the soul of integrity, not much more you can say about him than that. If I ever met a saint, he was one of them," Hesburgh says. "I don't think I would have had the patience to put up with that for more than a few minutes, literally. He put up with it day and night and was nothing less than heroic, as far as I'm concerned, how he took care of her."

144 | MR. NOTRE DAME

Yet more and more, he could not take care of himself. He remained in denial about the permanence of Elise's injuries, never allowing himself to face the truth. Instead, he dodged it the easiest way possible, accepting drinks he once turned down, staying late at parties he once left early.

At first, nobody noticed a change. Alcohol had always been part of the atmosphere at conventions and football games. Notre Dame fans in airports and hotel lobbies always wanted to buy drinks for Moose. He happily indulged, though he controlled his consumption, watering down his drinks or discreetly discarding them when they were still half-full. That control disappeared in the wake of the accident, eventually becoming too obvious to ignore.

✦ ✦ ✦

Krause remained a prominent figure on the Notre Dame athletic scene and beyond. He oversaw the rapid expansion of the department, from the addition of intramural and varsity sports to the construction of the Athletic and Convocation Center to expand and enhance facilities for both. He and Eleanor VanDerHagen became the first occupants of the building in the summer of 1968. Notre Dame even assigned an assistant athletic director, in a roundabout way, to help manage the increasing workload.

Colonel Jack Stephens, a former director of Notre Dame's ROTC program, became an administrative assistant in the football office after his retirement from the Army in 1968. A commander of a regiment of more than six thousand infantrymen in the South Pacific during World War II, Colonel Stephens earned three Bronze Stars, the Silver Star, the Legion of Merit and the Purple Heart.

He spent much of the 1950s as a military attaché in India and four years at the Pentagon before taking over Notre Dame's ROTC program in 1964. At a party marking his retirement from the Army, Hesburgh offered him the opportunity to work in the football office. But the colonel's curmudgeonly personality clashed with the coaching staff, and he was moved upstairs as assistant athletic director, the first—and last—appointed during Krause's tenure.

Krause and Colonel Stephens were as outwardly different as two people could be. As diminutive as he was domineering, the Colonel considered anyone taller than 5-foot-6 "a pituitary case." With a personality as cool on the surface as Krause's was warm, Colonel Stephens guarded his boss' open door and generous heart against budget complaints and ticket requests. "If Ed was a woman, he'd be a whore," the Colonel often chided, "because he can't say no." As NCAA regulations expanded exponentially, Krause—more comfortable with handshake agreements than handbooks—deferred the details of compliance. Colonel Stephens made sure Notre Dame followed the letter of the law; Krause made sure the Irish never strayed from the spirit of sportsmanship.

A mutual respect and deep friendship developed. Krause admired the Colonel's decorated military career, and the Colonel respected Krause's loyalty to family, faith, country and Notre Dame. Not that they ever told each other that. They never stopped trading barbs and practical jokes, the best way they knew to express their feelings for each other.

As a career military man, Colonel Stephens considered Krause his superior officer and served him accordingly, even making sure a cup of hot coffee awaited him when he arrived in the morning. Krause enjoyed confounding the Colonel's precise sense of timing. Occasionally he would slip into his office fifteen or twenty minutes earlier than usual. "Where's my coffee, Colonel?" would be the first words heard from him all day. "What's taking so long? Let's go. Move. We've got a department to run. There's no time for this dillydallying." And the Colonel would spring into action, albeit with a few epithets he would use only with a civilian boss. Krause just sat back and puffed on a cigar with a smug smile.

When Krause and Colonel Stephens started sharing a room on football road trips, the bickering about who snored the loudest became part of their routine. Krause kept him up all night with his snoring, the Colonel said, so one night he tiptoed over to his bed and kissed him on the cheek. Krause then spent the night alert for the Colonel's next move, while he slept soundly in silence. That story represents not only the affable antagonism of their relationship, but also its intimacy. There was an unspoken but understood admiration between them, almost like spouses, which would inspire the Colonel's loyalty when it would be needed most.

Still popular on the speaking circuit, Krause continued to accept many invitations, from university functions to athletic banquets to religious retreats. Twice in three years after Elise's accident, he traveled to Europe at the request of U.S. Army chaplains to speak to the Military Council of Catholic Men.

On one of the trips, an Air Force general in the audience offered Krause a ride after his speech. He asked Krause to give another talk, which led to another, and then another, cutting short his planned side trip to visit a friend in Luxembourg. "Air Force Steals Army's 'Marine'" read the headline on an account of Krause's journey in the *South Bend Tribune*. From the Army retreat at Berchtesgaden, Krause spoke at Wiesbaden, Ramstein, Hahn and Bitgurg at the Air Force's request. "They treated me royally everywhere," Krause said, "and finally I got to Luxembourg about three days late."

Krause's speeches followed his familiar pattern, sweetened with humor to make the serious point more palatable. In the wake of Elise's accident, the message of faith he delivered to the troops carried a special poignancy. He never mentioned his wife's accident and its aftermath, the burden he would later describe as "a veritable crucifixion."

> Getting to that faith described in sermons is going to take a lifetime and it's going to be a painful process. Faith isn't a blank

check on happiness. No one ever said that if you believe, the pain of being a human is just going to disappear. Faith isn't a back door out of the human condition. Faith doesn't change the facts of life. It just lets you see them in a different light. It lets you see into them and through them. Pains don't hurt less because you know there is a God. It's just that in their midst, you know that they aren't the whole story. Faith isn't a nothing now, everything later proposition, the one thing that used to be called 'pie in the sky when you die.' . . . Faith is saying yes to God, but the yes is said here and now, where the needs are, where the claims are, where the questions are asked, where God makes himself felt, where love is challenged.

Krause's demeanor did not betray the challenge he faced with Elise or within himself, but it revealed itself dangerously over time. His weight ballooned to 280 pounds and he developed an irregular heartbeat. One hot summer afternoon, after Elise had chastised him about trimming the hedges next to their house, he went to work. He started sweating profusely and breathing heavily, the top of the hedges leaning diagonally from his steadily drooping posture. "That was one of the first indications that he was starting to have heart trouble," Mary says.

Doctors prescribed medication to steady his irregular heart rhythm, but with the amount of alcohol he poured into his system, it became a nearly lethal combination. *South Bend Tribune* sports editor Joe Doyle, who often occupied the barstool next to Krause, recalled one typical binge. In New York for Frank Leahy's induction into the College Football Hall of Fame in 1969, Doyle, Krause and friends partied long into the night despite an early-morning flight home. They stopped drinking barely long enough for a couple hours of sleep.

"Even though we were out half the night, until three o'clock in the morning, and got up at six to get to LaGuardia, well, Moose says we've got to have a little toddy," Doyle says. "There's one of these lit-tle hole-in-the-wall bars [in the airport]. Moose got a Bloody Mary and he says, 'Well, that tastes just like another one,' before he even got the first one up. And I had two Bloody Marys with him and got him onto the plane."

Krause ordered two more drinks from the stewardess after takeoff, "and then some sonuvabitch Notre Dame fan knew Moose and got two for Moose," Doyle says. "He's got six or seven drinks by the time we get to Cleveland."

After another couple rounds in a bar at the Cleveland airport, Krause staggered to their connecting flight to Fort Wayne, where he had such a good time in the bar that he nearly missed the final leg of their trip back to South Bend. "Finally, I was just shepherding him," Doyle says. "We got to Fort Wayne, Jesus Christ, I had to go back in and get Moose and practically drag him to get him on the goddamn plane."

After they arrived in South Bend, Krause told Doyle they had to stop in to see Louie, the bartender at the airport. Because they were old friends from all of Krause's travels, Louie gave his buddy a drink about twice as stiff as he normally poured them. Doyle also had one or two more before convincing Krause they needed to head home, though they had left New York so early it was barely after noon.

"I had my car at the airport and drove Moose home and we get to Moose's, you know, functional. I know that he had the equivalent of ten to fifteen drinks at that time," Doyle says. "Moose wanted me to come in with him. I knew why he wanted me to come in." To insulate him from the wrath of Elise, not that he needed the help. As adept as Krause had become at caring for her, and as patient as he was with her outbursts, he also learned how to run an end-around when necessary.

"Mother," Krause said in his most delicate tone. "Father has been out all night. We put the old coach in the Hall of Fame, and Father's got a very important meeting on the campus at five o'clock, so Father's going to take a little beddy-bye." With that, Doyle says, "he tottered up the stairs and went to sleep."

✦ ✦ ✦

Krause's input in those important meetings became more and more inconsistent during a time of rapid expansion and philosophical changes about postseason play and coeducation. Notre Dame administrators seriously considered accepting a bowl invitation in 1969 for the first time since Rockne took the Four Horsemen to the 1925 Rose Bowl. Rumors about this impending change in university policy swirled and bowl representatives eagerly, if warily, courted Notre Dame. Its long-standing policy against postseason play cautioned the men in the candy-colored blazers not to get too excited. A change in the academic calendar made it possible and Notre Dame agreed to play in the Cotton Bowl against Texas.

Father Joyce and Colonel Stephens worked out the details while Krause served as a liaison with wining and dining bowl representatives who wanted Notre Dame in their game. Ultimately, the Cotton Bowl's soft sell—and the promise of No. 1 ranked Texas as the opponent—made the difference.

Krause participated in the bowl negotiations, but his condition increasingly limited his capacity to meet the demands of his job. Rumblings began about replacing him, although his popularity in college athletic circles still allowed him to make a valuable, if intangible, contribution. Krause kept Notre Dame on amiable terms with its competitors, but some wondered how much longer that benefit would outweigh the burden of his alcoholism.

Colonel Stephens ensured the athletic department ran with military efficiency, keeping tight controls on the budget, coordinating schedules, organizing contracts and keeping Krause's more frequent drunken episodes as quiet as possible. "The Colonel actually took over, in my opinion, and ran the place," Phil Krause says. "Because there were times when he was incapacitated."

Krause's drinking became increasingly difficult to hide. When he ambled into the faculty club on campus, professors would switch from beer to scotch or gin, because they knew Moose would be buying. Calls from bartenders at Woodward's Tavern or the Capri Restaurant to Krause's home or office became more common, making a single phrase as familiar as it was distressing.

"Somebody's got to come pick him up."

Krause did not always have a ride home. After a few drinks in the bar after a round of golf at South Bend Country Club left him happily tipsy, he often drove along the busy west side gateway into town. It concerned Krause's children that, at best, he might injure himself driving in that condition, and at worst, inflict the same pain on another family that had triggered his own descent into alcoholism.

They tried to confront him with photographs and stories about his slurred speech and sloppy appearance. In the grips of the disease, he denied everything, as if the alcohol had literally erased his memory. "We couldn't get to him as a family," Phil says. "He'd just say, 'That's not me.'"

For years, Krause never had an external reason to acknowledge his problem. Colonel Stephens' protective presence kept him ignorant of the pressure some influential figures exerted to replace him. A group approached Parseghian, insisting he step in as athletic director. "Moose is in bad shape," they told him. "You've got to take over. We're going to push for that."

Parseghian always had more than a working relationship with Krause. They shared a deeper, unspoken bond because they each endured a family member's illness. Parseghian's daughter, Karan, had been diagnosed with multiple sclerosis. In his time of crisis, Parseghian received sympathy and support from Krause. When influential factions maneuvered to remove Krause, Parseghian returned the favor.

"I remember this vividly," Parseghian says. "I was a bit offended by it. They will remain anonymous, but they were people in positions of authority, people that could influence the decision."

"Our job is to get him well," the coach told them, "he's too good a guy."

Like many others, Parseghian delicately tried to broach the subject with Krause, but he brushed it off. No accident ever shook Krause from his stupor to discover any tangible damage he had done as a result of his drinking. If anything, alcohol brought the warm, jovial side of his personality closer to the surface, making him even more popular, more human, among the masses of fans who greeted him everywhere with a hearty "Mooooooooooooooose!" Even family and friends found his demeanor endearing after a few drinks.

"I remember trying to help him out when he'd come back. He'd be laughing with us. He'd be playing pranks on us," Phil says. "One time, he got stuck in the shower and he was just laughing."

A confluence of factors awakened him. Compounding his heart condition with up to three bottles of scotch a day, Krause flirted dangerously with death. Visiting Parseghian one winter at his vacation home on Marco Island, Florida, Krause leaned over to tee up his ball on the tenth hole and collapsed. He was unconscious as Parseghian and their playing partners struggled to lift him. "Once we got his head up, he regained consciousness," Parseghian says. "I took him right up to Naples in my car. Our facilities on the island were not very good at the time. I remember him in the car. He was the same old Moose, even though he had just had a heart attack.

"Once he got onto the table and the doctor came in to examine him, I know he was worried, but that calmness remained. There was no panic. I don't think I ever saw him in a panicked state." When the doctor decided to keep Krause overnight for observation, Parseghian's biggest concern was how to explain his absence to Elise.

"What should we tell her?" Parseghian asked.

"Just tell her that I'm getting a free examination at the hospital," Krause instructed him. "She'll love that."

Parseghian and his wife, Katie, related his white lie at dinner and braced for an outburst.

"Oh, that's wonderful," Elise said. She especially liked the fact that this impromptu physical would be free, Krause's calming influence on his wife evident even from a hospital bed miles away.

"So here was Moose, he knew her right to the T; he knew exactly what the situation was," Parseghian says. "Even when he was having this attack, he was just the same old Moose."

That second heart scare reinforced the Krause family's fear that he would not be able to sustain his dangerous lifestyle much longer. If an accident would not kill him, his overburdened heart would. Anger began to well up inside them, their empathy for the pain he had endured diminishing with each drink he consumed to dull it. Still dealing with Elise's enduring disability, they felt their father's drinking would also cheat them out of his companionship. "We didn't think he'd last another five years the way he was going, so we got prepared for the end," Phil says. "That's the way we looked at it, because we didn't expect him to clean himself up."

Friends rallied to offer their help. Deacon Tom Hamilton, an executive at WNDU-TV in South Bend and a recovering alcoholic himself, encouraged Krause to enter Alcoholics Anonymous. Colonel Stephens tried to break him down like a private in basic training. Father Ed made an emotional plea on a summer visit home in the early 1970s. Citing all the sacrifices Mary and Phil had made to help take care of Elise, he confronted his father with the fundamental unfairness of the burden his drinking added to their shoulders.

"I'm going to interrupt my doctoral work and come home and take care of you and Mother," Father Ed said. "Mary and Phil have done their part. Now, it's my turn. I'll follow you around, that's all, I'll just follow you around and get you home safely at night."

That served as a sobering slap to the face, the truth seeping through for the first time.

"Give me one more chance," Krause said with tears welling in his eyes. "I only need one more chance."

He almost did not get that chance. Krause suffered a massive heart attack that left him unconscious on an operating table at St. Joseph's Hospital, requiring shock treatments to survive. In town for a visit at the time, Mary saw her father's lifeless body jerk with each jolt. A flat line on the monitor revealed the futility of the procedure. A doctor told her any increase in the voltage would kill him. Certain she would watch her father die otherwise, she signed a form authorizing them to give him the highest dosage they had ever administered. Krause's body jumped two feet and fell back down to the table, the blips representing his heartbeat beginning again.

His eyes blinked open as Mary approached him. Burn marks from the paddles, like the imprint of an iron left on a shirt too long, blistered his chest. Pregnant with her first child, Mary appealed to him as grandfather-to-be.

"You nearly died," she said, her voice at once scornful and tearful, husky with pent up anxiety and tinged with relief that she even had an opportunity to speak to him again. "If you don't do something, you won't live to see your grandchild."

Like Father Ed, she promised to move back home, leaving her own life behind as long as necessary to care for her parents. Krause had lost control of himself; how could he tend to Elise's increasing needs? Mary told him she could no longer watch from afar as her father's self-inflicted deterioration sped toward death. If he could not clean up by himself, she would be there day and night to see that he did.

Krause thought of his first-born son and his pride that he had entered the priesthood; he thought of Phil, another Notre Dame man in the family; he thought of Elise, who spent twenty-nine years loving and caring for him and how desperately she needed his love and care now; he looked up at his pregnant daughter with her mother's determined eyes, her angry pledge ringing in his ears, and he vowed, "You'll never have to do that."

✦ ✦ ✦

Krause began attending Alcoholics Anonymous meetings. He commiserated with Tom Hamilton and other friends and colleagues on campus struggling to recover from the same disease. Colonel Stephens kept a watchful eye on him in the first months of his sobriety to assure that he stayed that way. He did, eventually hosting Alcoholics Anonymous meetings in his office. He sought out and offered counsel to other people who appeared to have a problem. When Krause publicly acknowledged his battle with alcoholism, people from all walks of life began to attend the meetings he and Hamilton organized, his recovery inspiring a cross section of the community.

Like many of the biggest events in Krause's life, even his alcoholism became fodder for humor. Bill Kastelz, writing in the *Jacksonville Times-Union*, noted in an affectionate column about Krause and his recovery that Notre Dame's difficult football schedules looked like they were set up by someone with a drinking problem. "They were," Kastelz wryly noted.

Though Krause took his problem seriously, he never took himself seriously, never considered his disease a stigma to be hidden or a blemish on his reputation. He discussed it publicly—appearing before the National Alcoholism Council in Washington and joining the South Bend chapter's board of directors.

He intervened privately on behalf of anyone whose path he crossed who needed help. Krause had a discreet and gentle way of approaching friends and colleagues in the grip of alcoholism. Many others called him, asking for advice.

As many as fifteen people each week attended the AA meetings in Krause's office, creating a support system that helped them all stay sober. Krause opened each meeting with a prayer that revealed the simplicity and difficulty of their challenge.

> God, grant us the serenity to accept the things we cannot change, the courage to change the things we can, and the wisdom to know the difference.
>
> Today is the tomorrow about which we worried yesterday. Now is our only chance to make the most of it. Until it arrived we could do nothing about it, and after it is gone we can do nothing about it. Today is the only day about which we need to be concerned. Please help us. Amen.

They worked through the steps of the program, admitting their weakness, denying their excuses, taking a moral inventory of their lives, making amends with people they hurt and pledging to help others with the same affliction.

"I was profoundly and deeply impressed by the sensitivity, the faith, the richness of the exchanges of the people from the university and South Bend, priests, professors, truck drivers, businessmen, factory workers, who didn't mind meeting in Moose's office," Father Ed says. "These AA meetings were as rich, as moving, as any other group I've ever been with."

Mr. Notre Dame

N THE AUTUMN OF 1974, ARA PARSEGHIAN INFORMED
his bosses that he would resign, effective at the end of
the season. He had endured the indescribable pressure
of leading the Notre Dame football program for more than a decade.
In Krause's opinion, only Rockne and Leahy had handled it as well.
Winning two national titles in tumultuous times, Parseghian satisfied the
hunger for victory without tarnishing Notre Dame's golden reputation.
A second national championship in 1973 established Parseghian as a
bona fide Irish legend, but the heat of the spotlight had done its
inevitable damage.

An offseason incident involving six players and a woman in a dorm
room after hours inspired some salacious fodder for the press and contributed to the increasing strain Parseghian felt. The woman called
police and accused the players of rape, but never filed a formal complaint. Nevertheless, the players at least had violated Notre Dame's
sacrosanct parietals rule governing when men and women could be in
each other's rooms. They were suspended from school for a year. Five

were readmitted the following year and one transferred, but the episode scarred Parseghian.

"Ara had always worried about the actions of every staff and team member," Tom Pagna writes in *Notre Dame's Era of Ara*. "It was more than just pride with him that no blemish, no tragic episode, no defamation to Notre Dame would ever result from anything he was connected with, but now he wore the look of anguish."

Krause considered it an individual problem, not institutional, an isolated incident that did not reflect Parseghian's control of the team. "The way you evaluate coaches is not wins and losses, but the way his players respect him," Krause said in a *Chicago Tribune* article years later, "but it's emotional, no question about it." He never felt as emotionally attached to a coach as he did to Parseghian.

That's why Krause visited the coach's home late one night with Father Joyce, hoping to convince him to reconsider his resignation, which had yet to be made public. "Take a year off," Krause said, equating his idea to a professor's sabbatical. "Get away. Relax. We'll name an interim coach and you can come back refreshed."

Parseghian insisted his batteries had been depleted past the point of recharging. Pagna described how the coach's demeanor changed toward the end of his tenure: "Ara was morose, less dynamic and energetic than I ever remembered. . . . He was tired and stooped, almost totally preoccupied. Where his radiant eyes formerly pierced your mind, they now drifted in a distant gaze."

Krause saw the same physical evidence, but he could not bring himself to accept Parseghian's departure. "Look, I don't want you to resign," Krause said. "You can become the athletic director. I'll step down and then you can be athletic director and football coach."

"Moose, that's not why I'm stepping down," a stunned Parseghian said. "I have no interest in the athletic directorship."

"If you're not ready for it now," Krause said, "just tell me when you are and I'll step aside."

Parseghian and Krause had endured so much together since they became colleagues more than a decade earlier. Like an older brother, Krause had eased Parseghian's worries about the job; he offered comfort and perspective in defeat; he beamed with pride in Parseghian's considerable accomplishments.

They each faced personal trials that bonded them and shared extraordinary experiences on and off the field. Parseghian acted directly on Krause's behalf whenever he needed help, either in the sudden aftermath of a heart attack or during the slow and more insidious deterioration of his alcoholism. Through all those highs and lows, wins and losses, they never exchanged an angry word. "Even as volatile as I was," Parseghian says, "in those eleven years we never had an argument. That was a tribute to him, not me."

When Parseghian's departure became official, Krause wept at the press conference. He considered the moment one of Notre Dame's greatest losses, the reason he tried so hard to postpone it, even if it meant leaving the job he loved. Krause had received many lucrative offers over the years, but they never tempted him. Eight to ten times his salary, which never exceeded $30,000 a year at Notre Dame, and professional prestige could not lure him away. To keep Parseghian, he would have gladly stepped aside.

"He was very distraught when Ara decided to retire," Joyce says. "He did everything in his power to encourage him to stay, including offering him his own job. He was sincere about that."

"Out of the clear blue sky," Parseghian says, marveling at Krause's offer. "That demonstrates what kind of a guy he was."

Swirls of gray salted Parseghian's hair and deep lines creased his face, the toll of the tireless intensity he brought to his job. He had navigated an era of student unrest, deftly giving his players the freedom to question authority without losing the respect for it that a successful football program required. If they attended class and fulfilled their obligations to their teammates and coaches, Parseghian told them, he would not question their involvement in antiwar demonstrations or other student protests. If they honored their commitments, he would respect their point of view, however they expressed it.

That philosophy began with Hesburgh and filtered through the entire university leadership. They wanted to allow a certain amount of student freedom without yielding on their fundamental ideals. Krause, always politically and socially conservative though seldom vocal on the subject, had his own way of dealing with long hair and laissez-faire attitudes about drugs that he disdained. He kept a shaggy wig in his office and whenever an unkempt student stopped by he pulled it out and plopped it on top of his head—"How do you think I look with hair like yours?"—half-joking, but trying to make a point about the importance of appearance.

When word got around about an athlete indulging too much in the recreational diversions common among students of that era, Krause would discreetly summon him. He spoke about the dangers of drugs and alcohol, about commitment to family, friends and teammates. He spoke emphatically, his gravely baritone conveying authority. Yet he also spoke with empathy, his well-known personal experience conveying understanding.

That allowed Krause to maintain a connection with the student body at a time when, on the surface, they appeared to have little in common. He corresponded with his son, Father Ed, then a professor at Stonehill College in Massachusetts, about ways to reach across a generation gap that seemed more distant than ever.

When students in the crowd at football and basketball games directed vulgarities at opponents and officials, it confused Krause as much as it angered him. He could not understand how they considered such behavior encouraging to their team. Yet the pangs of his own embarrassing incidents in the past tempered his disapproval. Krause appealed to their sense of pride in the school they claimed to support, urging them to act in a manner at once spirited and respectful.

Krause had absolute faith in the institutions that defined his life—the Catholic Church, Notre Dame, marriage, the military. He believed in the values they espoused and the ideals they pursued, even if people did not always live up to them. He understood the inevitability of human weakness—indeed, he vividly experienced it—and never questioned the integrity of an institution he admired because of the failings of an individual.

It pained him most when people lamented their lack of faith in the Catholic Church, decrying it as a haven of hypocrites who did not practice what they preached. He heard it most often from disaffected students who grew up with the traditions but discarded them because they felt religious and lay leaders did not live up to the ideals of Jesus. Instead of debating them, Krause had a simple, prepared response that made his point. "As an outsider," he would ask, "how do you feel about the human race?"

✦ ✦ ✦

In the twilight of Krause's tenure at Notre Dame, the full sweep of his accomplishments, athletic and otherwise, began to come into focus. Krause's devotion and service to the Catholic Church was rewarded in 1975 with one of the highest honors a layman can receive. Terrence Cardinal Cooke inducted Krause into the Knights of Malta in a ceremony at St. Patrick's Cathedral in New York. "Was he proud of that," Eleanor VanDerHagen says. "He strutted with that cape and the hat that they wear."

In recognition for his lifelong commitment to the value of health and fitness, the City of Hope National Medical Center established an Edward W. Krause Medical Research Fellowship. The citation read: "The City of Hope, dedicated to the health and well-being of mankind, is proud to bestow upon Edward W. 'Moose' Krause, whose life has been devoted to the physical fitness of young people, its Spirit of Life Award."

Krause's career as a player and coach were worthy of induction into the National Basketball Hall of Fame in Springfield, Massachusetts. Though the memories had faded like the brittle, yellowed newspaper clippings that chronicled them, they remained vivid enough to be celebrated in 1976. They also highlighted how much had changed since the days Krause played.

He spent his last years at Notre Dame as a wise elder statesman, a fixture whose contributions could not be quantified, but to some, a man whose time had passed. He may have felt that way himself. A burgeoning NCAA bureaucracy, preening touchdown dances and acrobatic dunks made the games he played and the values he cherished seem almost archaic.

Perhaps because he had been so close to Parseghian, Krause never developed a close relationship with his successor, Dan Devine, despite a national championship in 1977. Flamboyant basketball coach Digger Phelps also brought great success to Notre Dame in the 1970s, but Krause never warmed to his flashy style.

Coeducational since 1972, Notre Dame had a women's sports program in its infancy, which Krause supported and helped initiate. Like many old-timers in college athletics, though, it made him uncomfortable. Krause considered the development of women's sports an important step forward—his granddaughter, Jill, would grow up to be a Notre Dame basketball player—but it contributed to the feeling that his way of doing business no longer applied.

Notre Dame's athletic department budget had grown from $500,000 annually to $4.5 million and counting during his tenure. That created myriad modern responsibilities, demanding an athletic director well-versed in a variety of fields and adaptable to constant change and explosive expansion.

"Now you have to have knowledge of entertainment and business and handle a wide range of things, including women's sports," Krause said. At age sixty-seven, after thirty-one years as athletic director, he announced his retirement. Virginia athletic director Gene Corrigan stepped in as his successor.

Krause's lame duck status was symbolized in the final football coaching change of his tenure. When Dan Devine resigned in 1980 after six seasons and a national championship, Krause lobbied for a young coach from Arkansas named Lou Holtz to replace him.

Instead, the coach from Moeller High School in Cincinnati, Gerry Faust, whose infectious enthusiasm for Notre Dame oozed from every pore, won the approval of Hesburgh and Joyce. As he had with Terry Brennan nearly thirty years earlier, Krause disagreed with the decision but publicly supported it and privately developed a close relationship with Faust despite his fruitless five years at the helm.

Faust's mediocre 30-26-1 record fell far short of expectations, and fans expressed vitriolic disapproval. Newspaper and magazine articles questioned his qualifications for the job. Krause tried to insulate Faust from the criticism, but it was too prevalent. Like every other Irish fan, Faust's record upset Krause, but the coach's passionate spirit and love for Notre Dame inspired him. In fact, in Krause's eyes, Faust embodied the value of sport itself. In his essay "Though the Odds Be Great: The Spirit of Notre Dame," Krause detailed his respect for the embattled coach:

> Gerry Faust lost more games than any other Notre Dame coach, but in his own way, and in the only way he could, he was true to the Notre Dame spirit. He challenged the fates and strove mightily. He gave all that he could, and when that wasn't enough, he stepped aside with dignity and grace. In

the worst of circumstances, when hounded and harassed by some of the press and dissatisfied alumni, he remained a gentleman and in control of himself, demonstrating again that we cannot only survive the trials and tests that come our way, but in some respects even thrive in their midst. In what really counts, he was far from broken—integrity, fairness, self-control, fortitude and stamina.

Tributes to Krause appeared regularly during his final year at the helm, attaching those same attributes and more to him. In the *Chicago Tribune*, columnist Dave Condon summed up Krause's legacy and described the void his retirement would create:

> They'll never forget Rock, The Gipper, The Four Horsemen, The Master or Ara. But as long as good sports pour down the thunder, the man they'll remember most vividly is Notre Dame's No. 1. He's the real legend.
>
> As students and sports chiefs, Knute Rockne and Frank "The Master" Leahy together were not on the Fighting Irish campus as long as No. 1 . . .
>
> No. 1 has walked past the Golden Dome for more seasons than the combined totals of George Gipp, the Four Horsemen and Ara Parseghian. He goes on, like a Dan Devine speech.

A Moose Krause Appreciation Fund, established to honor his loyal service to the university, raised $100,000 in less than two years, the retirement nest egg his salary never allowed him to save. He also received a Cadillac with a vanity "MOOSE K" license plate, a monthly box of cigars for life, a humidor to store them, and a lifetime membership at South Bend Country Club.

On May 2, 1981, a retirement roast attracted more than fifteen hundred friends and admirers to the Athletic and Convocation Center arena. "It is not only fitting that tonight's testimonial dinner will be held in the same place Notre Dame plays basketball but it is necessary," Wayne Fuson wrote in the *Indianapolis Star*. "There isn't anyplace else in South Bend big enough to hold the crowd which wants to pay him tribute."

Keith Jackson, one of the nation's most familiar voices on college football television broadcasts, served as the master of ceremonies. A head table of dignitaries from college sports and education, business and media, searched their own files full of familiar old jokes to skewer Moose in front of fifteen hundred friends and admirers. They found little they could apply to him. "It's kinda boring," Jackson intoned, "to roast a guy that everybody loves."

A few tried. Heisman Trophy winner Johnny Lujack opened with the catchy lead: "I can remember the first time that Moose was arrested in South Bend. The jailer woke him up the following morning and he says, 'Moose, you know you're in here for drinking.' So Moose says, 'Well, then let's get to it.'"

Once the applause died down after his introduction, Parseghian resorted to tweaking Krause's liberal attitude toward the rules of golf: "A man of great honesty and integrity, really, Moose is. But when it comes to golf, he's been known to nudge the ball in the rough, kick the ball out from behind some shrubs, and once in a while knock the ball away from a tree. Some fool out at South Bend Country Club had the audacity to ask Moose, 'What are you doing kicking the ball out from behind that tree?' And Moose said, very casually, without getting excited, 'I don't pay $120 a month out here at this country club to play from behind trees.' He's absolutely a mathematical genius when it comes to golf. He's a guy that yells 'Fore!', makes six and puts down five on his card."

Former Air Force Academy football coach Ben Martin found his roasting material in Krause's sterling reputation itself: "I understand he worked his way through here posing for holy pictures. In his free time, he worked as a freelance character witness."

Krause took advantage of the evening's light-hearted tone with a tongue-in-cheek retort to his roasters, hinting at imminent litigation for their slanderous remarks. "I've enjoyed the evening very thoroughly," Krause said, "except for some of the disgusting lies that have been told about me this evening. . . . As I tried to think of something to say about some of these disgusting people who told so many untruths, I thought of Plato, Aristotle, [but] if I spoke about them, they wouldn't understand. Therefore, I thought of a modern philosopher. I thought of the great Zygmont Pierre Czarobski, who said, 'A friend in need, is a pain in the ass.'

"Furthermore, for the benefit of these liars who were here earlier this evening. Do you know there was a recording of everything that was said here tonight? I've got a dozen lawyers. You'll have trouble the next few days, believe me."

Krause followed through on his threat through his lawyer, former Notre Dame star Creighton Miller. He circulated letters to Ara Parseghian, Johnny Lujack, former Fordham athletic director Pete Carlesimo, Ray Meyer and others, informing them of a $100,000 lawsuit for "defamation of character." Responses crossed in the mail for months, reprising the roast's needling tone in mock legalese:

I am in receipt of your letter dated May 15, 1981, indicating that there will be a pending defamation of character lawsuit filed against the author of this letter in the amount of $100,000. Through this communiqué, I wish to advise you that the Armenian Mafia is preparing a countersuit of $100,000,000. We don't fool around with chicken feed.

With regrets,
Ara Parseghian

I will pay an additional $100,000 to Mr. Krause if I can repeat my remarks on national television so that the whole country will know the despicable type of person you represent.

Prior to the Roast, my comments were edited by Pope John Paul II. His Holiness replied, "After investigating Moose Krause's background and carefully evaluating all the information relating particularly to his character, your remarks were extremely charitable bordering on Saintliness. I would personally judge Moose to be a Louse."

Suingly yours,

John C. Lujack, The Suee

I am eagerly looking forward to meeting you in court in the very near future. I visited with my lawyer (an Italian boy) and he advises me that after reviewing the transcript of the so-called Testimonial Dinner, he assures me that the truth was documented. My only regret is that I did not have sufficient time to expose you completely. Your requested retirement is indeed a great blessing to Notre Dame.

Truthfully yours,

Peter of the Carlesimos

Crusade for Truth Chairman

How can you defame a man's character when he doesn't have one?

Yours,

Ray Meyer

For all the humor that peppered the dinner and its aftermath, Hesburgh articulated the esteem for Krause never far from the surface of anyone's remarks. He recounted his respect for Krause, developed from their earliest encounters when Hesburgh, as the newly appointed executive vice president, entered the unfamiliar world of athletic administration:

> I was green as grass. My first job was to redo all the rules for intercollegiate athletics, about which I knew very little. Moose had been athletic director for all of two months at that point and we got together and we did those rules. I think I can tell you in all honesty that those rules are still in vigor today and that's part of the legend of Moose Krause.
>
> In his own person he symbolized the two things that have always symbolized athletics at this university under his care. One is that athletes are students and students are athletes. Four out of every five students in this university today, men and women, participate in athletics. As to the varsity sports that somehow have the limelight, let me tell you that under Moose Krause there has never been a major or a minor scandal, because he has always believed that athletes should graduate in four years in normal courses. He has always believed that the rule of the game should be, most of all, integrity, that there is no great honor in excellence, in great performance, even in national championships, if it's not linked to integrity of performance.
>
> I think, Moose, the greatest thing I must thank you for is not that we won all those national championships, not that we've had the thrill of so many great games, so many come-from-behind games, not that we've had so many All-Americans. But it has been done with class, and even more than class, it has been done with integrity. I don't know how many schools in this land can match that record, but then, how many schools in this land have had a Moose Krause at the helm for over thirty years?

✦ ✦ ✦

Krause remained actively involved in the Notre Dame athletic department, particularly during the pageantry of football season and other special occasions honoring the school's storied athletic history.

When President Ronald Reagan, who played George Gipp in *Knute Rockne All-American,* visited Notre Dame in 1988 to dedicate the new Rockne postage stamp, Krause played a prominent role in the ceremony. A *Chicago Tribune* reporter spotted him pacing backstage before his remarks on the rostrum with Reagan. Krause revered Reagan for his work to defeat Communism and it seemed natural that he would be nervous as he prepared to speak in his presence. That's not what worried him. "They gave me just two minutes," Krause said. "The only time I talked for two minutes or less was when I was mad." Despite his limited time, Krause managed to work in one of the day's most memorable lines, telling the crowd, "Never in our wildest dreams did we think George Gipp would become President of the United States."

Reagan's visit represented a culmination of Krause's career, revealing how the values of sports and spirituality he held so dear resonated even in the highest office in the land. Speaking in the midst of economic fears less than a year before he left office, Reagan echoed Krause's personal philosophy. Under the headline "PRESIDENT INVOKES THE ROCKNE CREED," the *New York Times* described Reagan's optimism in the face of those fears. It chronicled his confidence in an American will to win even when the outlook appeared bleak and concluded with his belief "that on or off the field, it is faith that makes the difference." Then, for good measure, Reagan reprised his role as George Gipp and threw a pass to reigning Heisman Trophy winner Tim Brown, connecting one era of Irish lore with another as Krause watched with pride at the president's side.

✦ ✦ ✦

Mary took care of Elise during Krause's busy autumn months at her home in Evanston, Illinois. Elise remained volatile and became more and more brittle as the years passed. Mary implored her father to put Elise in a nursing home, but he refused, no matter how fragile her condition became.

It took an accident to make it happen. While staying at Mary's house, Elise fell out of bed and broke her hip. Sandy Carrigan drove her back to South Bend, laid out on cushions in the back of a station wagon. Even Krause realized she needed the constant, professional care of a nursing home then and he relented.

Limping along the corridors of Cardinal Nursing Home by Elise's side, Krause's legs and his wife were not what they once were. His knees and hips showed their age and the effects of football, but Krause knew both he and Elise needed the exercise, however modest it may have been. When doctors insisted Elise get out of bed and walk, she often resisted or simply did not have the strength to stand. So Krause would carry her down the hall, her feet moving one in front of the other, but not touching the ground.

Once so strong in appearance and personality, Ed and Elise Krause experienced the last chapter of their lives together literally leaning on each other to make it from one end of the hall to the other. "We carry on together," Krause said, "but it has been a veritable crucifixion for both of us."

Krause's legs deteriorated to the point that he required hip replacement surgery in 1985. Elise's brother, Joe Linden, spent a few months in South Bend helping him recover, cooking meals and chauffeuring Krause to his appointments.

If Krause's body had aged the hard way of a former football player, his spirit, his dignity, his soul had grown stronger and more resolute. He earned his noble stature through the defeats he endured and the victories he willed in their wake. Krause considered his athletic experience the foundation for his persevering spirit. Looking back on his life, he felt his character formed on the field and the court, through the physical strain and mental challenge that accompanied the games he played.

"In the midst of it all, one gains, I think, a positive sense of what human involvement in the real world with all its fateful ambiguity and many harsh limits normally entails," Krause wrote. "It takes an unusual hardiness and stamina to challenge the fates, to risk everything in open competition, to face again and again the specter of defeat and public embarrassment until it no longer paralyzes you."

Krause viewed sports as an integral part of the pursuit of victory in life. He echoed Hesburgh's definition of a football season as a metaphor for the vagaries of existence. "It begins with warm and sunny days filled with optimism and hope," Hesburgh wrote, " [but] the sunshine wanes, the warmth diminishes, and optimistic hope is qualified by the hard lifelike realities of fierce competition, unexpected injuries, and the innate difficulty of sustained human effort."

As he aged, Krause developed an even deeper appreciation for the lessons of athletics. He always had attached educational and social significance to sports, but drawing from a lifetime of experience, he began to see them in a spiritual context as well:

> Anyone who has deeply lived the Notre Dame spirit and mystique instinctively thinks beyond the Saturday football victories to the larger, much more serious Easter victory of Jesus. . . . Even when we lose, as will often be the case in the real world, as Jesus surely does on the cross, still we are confident of a deeper, more serious victory, if we have followed the way of the Lord, a victory over all that corrupts or weakens us, a victory over all that compromises and complicates

our efforts. Because of our faith in God, and His promise to be with us, to sustain us, and finally to rescue us from the evils that afflict us, we never give up. And because we never give up, 'what though the odds be great or small,' Ole Notre Dame and her loyal sons and daughters will go on marching, marching onward to victory, the final victory, the only victory that really counts.

✦ ✦ ✦

Krause took advantage of the perks of his stature in many ways. He parked his Cadillac wherever it fit, the "MOOSE K" license plate a virtual permit to ignore street signs. He kicked his ball out from behind trees on the golf course. He puffed on his lifetime supply of pungent cigars beneath bright red signs that read: NO SMOKING. He even saw to it that his son accompanied him to bowl games with the Notre Dame traveling party as his personal "chaplain," as a Knight of Malta is entitled to have.

Of all the accolades bestowed on him, Krause's greatest achievement did not come with a cape or a medal or a testimonial banquet. It occurred during visiting hours at Cardinal Nursing Home, where he spoon-fed meals and sang to his ailing wife. "Your father has had many public successes in life," Hesburgh told Father Ed, "but nothing is more important in God's eyes than how he cared for your mother for all those years."

Philosopher Donald DeMarco writes, "Moose Krause was a giant and legend who had distinguished himself in a sport where giants were commonplace and at a school where legends were customary. Yet these marks of distinction, extraordinary as they are, take a distant second place when compared with the fidelity he showed to his wife."

Krause literally became DeMarco's textbook example of fidelity, alongside Winston Churchill's determination, Simone Weil's compassion and Edith Piaf's courage in *The Heart of Virtue: Lessons from Life and Literature Illustrating the Beauty and Value of Moral Character*. Krause considered his ongoing care for Elise nothing more than his opportunity to bring peace and comfort to her life—as she had done for him during their twenty-nine years together before the accident. He credited Elise with making the life he lived and loved possible.

Many people felt sorry for the sacrifices Krause made to be with Elise. He heard the whispers. They wished he would take a vacation from the mental burden of caring for his wife and absorbing her abuse, maybe spend his winters somewhere warm where he could golf and fish and forget for a few months.

Those closest to Krause urged him directly to do what so many acquaintances assumed he needed, to get away from the daily reminder of what he had lost. When Father Ed spent weeks at home in the summer, helping with Elise's care, he suggested his dad take off for some much-deserved relaxation.

"There's really no place I'd rather be than in that room with your mother," Krause said. "I know a lot of people feel sorry for me, but I'm the lucky one. I'm in the fortunate position of being able to extend care. That's the easy part. Mother has the hard part."

Krause considered being away from Elise a sacrifice, illustrating DeMarco's point that "fidelity is a more immediate expression of love than the desire for happiness. . . . The desire to be with the one whom one loves is more urgent and demanding than the desire for one's own happiness. Far from feeling sorry for Moose, those who knew him well both admired and envied him."

Krause not only honored the commitment he made to Elise "in sickness and in health," he reaffirmed it. Father Ed officiated a ceremony in August 1988 to honor his parents' fiftieth wedding anniversary. Krause wore a white tuxedo and dressed Elise in a long, blue gown. A small group of close friends and family attended. In the antiseptic atmosphere of Elise's room, Father Ed asked his father if he would take this woman to be his lawful . . .

"I do!" Elise blurted and the room erupted in laughter.

"Not yet, Mother," Krause said. "It's my turn."

✦ ✦ ✦

Krause still spent several hours a day in his office as athletic director emeritus—"emeritus," as he liked to joke, meaning "no paycheck"—his presence announced pungently by the scent of his cigars. He drank coffee and traded barbs with the Colonel, answered correspondence, greeted visitors, offered counsel to coaches and administrators, then drove his Cadillac onto Cartier Field to watch football practice.

His life had settled into a predictable, somewhat melancholy routine. He lived alone in a condominium along the St. Joseph River. Many of his friends had died or lived far away. He traveled to fewer away football games, usually only the bowls. Even Krause's happiest moments—his hours at the nursing home, at daily Mass or in his press box perch high above Notre Dame Stadium—brought twinges of sadness.

Visiting Elise reminded him of the pain in his personal life. Mass encouraged his faith in what awaited him in heaven, but it also reminded him of his mortality. Even football games had become reminders of the inevitable passage of time, the size and speed of the modern players dwarfing what he had been in his prime. In his booth with a dozen old friends during football games, the stories always drifted back to those days. Krause relished hearing familiar tales about Rockne and Leahy and telling a few of his own. It animated him, brightening eyes that had grown dark and damp from cigar smoke and sadness.

Friends coveted a seat in the press box with Krause. Bishop Joseph Crowley of the Fort Wayne–South Bend Diocese was always there, ready to pray for a miracle if necessary. Krause's old Marine Corps chaplain Father James Gannon made a game, usually when the weather was warm enough that they could golf for a day or two before. Legends of the Leahy era like Johnny Lujack, Creighton Miller, George Connor and his brother, Jack, always had a seat. Krause's children and grandchildren also absorbed the atmosphere of the booth when they were in town. It brimmed with nostalgia, spiced with a little armchair quarterbacking, inspiring Jack Connor, the author of *Leahy's Lads*, to write a poem called "In Heaven with Moose."

Moose gathers his friends and former players
To meet in that place up high
We cheer the team and we coach at times
You'd think it was do or die

Moose commands the booth and sets the drill
He keeps us all in line
He sets the tone that begins the same
"George, tell them about the time . . ."

The stories start and last all game
Ziggie's there and Leahy too
We laugh and cry as we reminisce
With the Golden Dome in view

We call the place Heaven it's got to be
We're up so high above
We tell our stories and share the laughs
We're with our Moose the one we love

✦ ✦ ✦

At least twice a day, Krause visited the nursing home to feed Elise and walk with her, singing her to sleep at night. He offered the same gentle care to Joe McArdle, Leahy's "Captain Bligh" of the 1940s, who had suffered a stroke and struggled to support his own weight. McArdle hated the nursing home, a proud, stubborn man reduced to following nurses' orders, which he often refused to do. Krause could convince him to eat. He could budge him from bed for brief walks, the two old coaches shuffling together, remembering when.

Krause also stopped in to see family friend Myrtle Adams almost every day, along with his children's third-grade teacher, Agatha Guendling. As her mental capacity decreased in her last years, Myrtle Adams often felt cold in her room and asked Krause for a sweater. He would pull one of several similar cardigans from her closet. Like a vaudeville routine, she would refuse it, so Krause would find another and she would shake her head at that one, too. He generally displayed about a dozen before she made a decision, usually a different one than the day before.

He displayed the same patience with her as he did with Elise, whose condition continued to deteriorate. Even Krause could see she had little time left, and he tried to make it peaceful for her. She lashed out at others, but he could calm her with soothing words or a song. He brought her greeting cards for special occasions, which he kept in a drawer at home and reused year after year because Elise could not remember them, though she loved receiving them.

Elise Krause died in March 1990. Krause placed a photograph of a young Elise on her tombstone at the family plot at Cedar Grove Cemetery on the Notre Dame campus. He wanted the world to remember her as he would, a vibrant and beautiful woman who supported and inspired him.

✦ ✦ ✦

Krause's friends noticed a change in his demeanor after Elise's death. He still teased them mercilessly and told old stories, but his mind seemed to drift and he started forgetting familiar details. Another hip replacement in 1991 slowed him even more. He spent his mornings in the pool at the Rolf's Aquatic Center on campus, walking in waist deep water on doctor's orders to strengthen his legs and his heart.

That operation and recuperation canceled Krause's planned trip to Lithuania in the summer of 1991. It would have been his first trip to his ancestral land since his athletic mission in 1935. He also planned to visit Rockne's birthplace in Voss, Norway.

Krause especially looked forward to returning to a Lithuania finally free of Soviet shackles. After the fall of the Communist bloc, Lithuania quickly achieved prominence in international basketball. They made an inspiring run to a bronze medal in the 1992 Olympics in Barcelona, defeating the "Unifed Team" of their former Soviet teammates by 37 points in the European qualifier.

That same summer, a dream that had driven Krause for years finally came true. Though he never earned induction into the College Football Hall of Fame because he had not been a first-team All-American, the South Bend Chapter of the Hall's National Football Foundation had been named in Krause's honor for years. In 1989, he had received the NFF's prestigious "Distinguished American Award" for his lifelong contributions to the game. What Krause wanted more than all those honors was to have the Hall of Fame itself in his home-town of South Bend.

Its location outside Cincinnati had not been profitable and Krause lobbied the NFF tirelessly to move it to South Bend. Word reached him while golfing with Moose Krause Chapter president Bill Starck in July 1992 that South Bend would be the Hall of Fame's new home. A hole-in-one would not have made him happier. "He was jumping up and down like a kid," Starck says. "He just went bananas."

"It's the best news I've gotten since Father [Edward] Sorin first camped out at Notre Dame," Krause told *South Bend Tribune* sports editor Bill Moor. "Better yet, it was the best news since [Alexis] Coquillard first settled in what become South Bend."

Krause had an extra spring in his step in the office, where he and Colonel Stephens remained cranky compatriots. They had become so close that Krause arranged for two extra plots in Cedar Grove Cemetery for the Colonel and his wife to be buried beside him and Elise. As Krause approached eighty, he realized he needed to be prepared for that inevitability. Not that he resigned himself to it. That would have been against his nature. Krause continued to live as actively as possible for a broken-down old athlete. He golfed regularly, though his game had weakened like his legs—all the more reason to apply his liberal interpretation of the rules. He never missed Mass or football practice, and he remained active in a variety of community projects. Once a month, he even had a date. Krause accompanied the widows of former athletic department officials to dinner at the University Club.

His presence at football weekend functions provided a concrete connection to the past at a school that basked in its history. Krause seldom gave speeches anymore, but he remained a fixture at luncheons and pep rallies, a living tribute to the Notre Dame tradition.

There also was more tangible proof of Krause's lasting contribution to Notre Dame. Athletic director Dick Rosenthal negotiated a five-year $35 million television contract with NBC to broadcast all Irish home football games. It echoed Notre Dame's push for institutional freedom in the infancy of television and also rewarded Krause's long-standing commitment to challenging schedules. "The television contract is certainly a product of that tradition," Rosenthal says. "There are other great teams in America, but nobody had the consistent, week after week schedule."

NBC got its money's worth on November 14, 1992, when Penn State visited Notre Dame Stadium. A steady snowfall blanketed the field and created a magical atmosphere. Neither team could establish much momentum in the slippery conditions and the group gathered "in heaven with Moose" fidgeted as the game built toward its breathtaking climax.

All the air seemed to go out of the booth when Penn State scored late in the game to take a 16-9 lead. Father Ed volunteered to leave early to pull Krause's car up to the gate for the ride home. He missed one of the most memorable finishes in Irish history in the process.

Notre Dame scored a late touchdown on a tense fourth-down play and decided to go for a two-point conversion to win with twenty seconds left. Quarterback Rick Mirer rolled to his left, then back across the field to his right, looking for an open receiver through the falling flakes. He spotted Reggie Brooks drifting across the back of the end zone and lofted a pass toward the corner. Brooks dove and somehow wrapped his hands around the wet, cold ball to secure the 17-16 win.

Defeating Penn State propelled the Irish into a Cotton Bowl meeting against Texas A&M. Krause pulled out his ten-gallon hat, a favorite souvenir from previous Cotton Bowl games, and wore it around the office in anticipation of another trip to Dallas.

Krause had that hat on three weeks later as he left the athletic department Christmas party on December 10. He enjoyed the dinner and had a couple cups of coffee as he sat away from the crowd, greeting a steady stream of friends and colleagues who approached him and the Colonel. "All the ladies were bringing him a plate of food," Rosenthal says. "Everybody was coming by and he was holding forth." As the music started and dancing began, Krause slipped out.

Sometime in the early morning hours of December 11, as he slept, the big heart that lived and loved so much finally stopped. Rosenthal's assistant athletic director, Joe O'Brien, interrupted an early-morning meeting to break the news to his boss. "Don't ask me why," Rosenthal says, "but when I saw the look on Joe's face, I knew what had happened."

Excusing himself from his meeting, Rosenthal drove over to Krause's condo, where he still lay in bed, wearing blue silk pajamas and a big smile. When Colonel Stephens arrived and saw him in that peaceful pose, the crusty old military man sat beside his best friend and cried.

News of Krause's death cast a pall across the Notre Dame campus, among the co-workers who knew him well and the students who knew him only by reputation. A palpable sense of loss also coursed through the South Bend community and rippled across the country anywhere his presence had been felt.

In the *New York Times,* his obituary carried the headline, "Ed Krause, 79; The 'True Legend' of Notre Dame." It quoted Gerry Faust, who echoed Dave Condon in the *Chicago Tribune* a decade before, placing Krause on a higher pedestal than the Gipper, Rockne and the Four Horsemen in Irish athletic lore. A billboard appeared in downtown South Bend in the days after Krause's death with an illustration of the Golden Dome in one corner and a one word salute: "MOOSE."

December 15, 1992, dawned steel gray and still, a frigid drizzle dampening the Notre Dame campus. Perhaps the greatest-ever gathering of Notre Dame athletic history paid their respects to Moose Krause in a stately funeral at the Basilica of the Sacred Heart. Not since Knute Rockne's memorial service more than sixty years earlier had such a celebrated collection of Irish athletes and administrators assembled. They came together to bid farewell to one of their best friends and greatest legends, the last remaining link between the tradition Rockne created and its modern heirs, the man who did as much to ennoble Notre Dame athletics as anyone in its rich history.

More than fifty clergymen, including two bishops and the entire university hierarchy, filled the altar for a ceremony that was solemn, but not somber. Ara Parseghian, one of six aging and ailing pallbearers, joked that Colonel Stephens may have done one of the worst recruiting jobs in school history in assembling the group who carried Krause's casket. Lou Holtz was so slight, he looked like a strong wind could knock him off his feet. George Kelly, Dick Rosenthal, George Connor and Parseghian could barely support themselves on their unsteady legs, much less the weight of Moose and his legend. And the Colonel himself, as his friends often reminded him, was so short his feet didn't touch the ground. "Moose in the casket," Parseghian says, "was in better shape than any of us."

Krause would have been moved to see so many people who represented his life's true loves—family, faith and football—honor him with such reverence. Nothing would have made him more proud, though, than to hear the eulogy delivered by his own son, the priest Krause himself never became:

> We are here this morning to respect and honor a gentle giant, the memory and work of my dear father and his generation. . . . He showed us again how to get along with one another, how to be faithful and loyal to the basics, to the ordinary, to the game as a game and its inherently humorous character, while yet striving to excel and be our best . . .
>
> He had a fisherman's simplicity, a child's innocence, an almost naive generosity. He gave largely, freely, easily, to his wife, to his children, family and friends, to coaches, colleagues and co-workers, even strangers and enemies . . .
>
> My father lived life the way he played ball: he never gave up, he never stopped trying. In religious terms, he was faithful. He was loyal. It wouldn't be important that he, like Peter

in the Gospel, may not always have succeeded. Jesus himself, of course, by purely worldly standards could only be counted a failure. No, what is important is that he, coach that he was, never stopped playing with all his heart and bulk. He fought, as Paul says in the epistle, to the finish line, right up to the final whistle, a Notre Dame trait if ever there was one.

At Cedar Grove Cemetery along Notre Dame Avenue at the edge of the campus, Krause was laid to rest beside his wife. With collars turned up against the cold, the mourners remained in silence for an awkward moment after the ceremony ended, unable to let go of this piece of their past. As if out of the mist, a song began. Father Hesburgh sang the opening words slowly and softly—so softly that only those standing near him could identify him as the source—and soon everyone joined in the impromptu farewell serenade:

> Cheer, cheer for old Notre Dame
> Wake up the echoes cheering her name
> Send a volley, cheer on high
> Shake down the thunder from the sky
> What though the odds be great or small
> Old Notre Dame will win over all
> While her loyal sons are marching
> Onward to victory

✦ ✦ ✦

Notre Dame football players wore "MOOSE" decals to honor his memory in the Cotton Bowl three weeks after his death. They placed them between the screws attaching the face mask to the helmet, an area that absorbs the brunt of the force when linemen collide, the physical fury Krause loved most about the game. Even in his prime, he could not have competed with the agile behemoths on the field that raw day in Dallas. But Edward "Moose" Krause, in life and in legend, with the memory of his emotional funeral still fresh, towered over the young men carrying on the tradition he worked a lifetime to preserve. He towers still.

About the Author

JASON KELLY COVERS NOTRE DAME FOOTBALL FOR THE *South Bend Tribune.* He lives with his wife, Kara, in South Bend, Indiana.